The Sixty-Year Caucasian War

THE SIXTY-YEAR CAUCASIAN WAR

BY ROSTISLAV FADEEV

TRANSLATED BY HARKO SKED

ANTELOPE HILL PUBLISHING

CONTENTS

General Overview   1

Muridism   13

Conquest of the Caucasus   47

Conclusion   99

GENERAL OVERVIEW

L ast September, Russia could hardly believe its eyes when it read Prince Baryatinsky's telegraphic dispatches to the tsar, which informed him "that the eastern Caucasus is subdued from the Caspian Sea to the Georgian Military Road," that "Shamil has been taken and sent to St. Petersburg"; Russian society knew, however dimly, that lately the situation in the Caucasus was going well, but did not expect such a rapid outcome yet.

The Caucasian War had gone on for sixty years. Russia had become accustomed to the idea that this state of affairs was natural and could last virtually forever, especially as the Caucasus region had remained in the shadows for about half a century, and the public opinion of it stemmed from a handful of stories and the accounts of people who traveled to take in the waters of Pyatigorsk. In 1845, the newspapers began to publish accounts of the relations, but they could only enlighten the matter for a person already familiar with the Caucasus. Considering the extraordinary variety of this vast country, the most mature experience gained on one of its military theaters did not necessarily afford a correct judgment on another; from a distance everything merged into one murky image, the most radical changes in the situation were smoothed out, and the thinking Russian man who was not personally familiar with the Caucasus could not connect the divergent events and arrived, in his search for solutions to this problem, at the most improbable conclusions. Our society, for the most part, did not even understand why the state worked so hard, made so many sacrifices, to conquer these mountains. Although the countries comprising the Caucasian Governorate were rich in natural resources and situated in a geographical position that would allow for remarkable future development, from a purely economic perspective they could not repay the sacrifices made to gain possession of them. It was not an economic question that was being decided in the Caucasus. Understandably, this issue, lacking a straightforward angle, remained confusing to most of the public. At most, the conquest of the eastern mountains satisfied Russian patriotism as a victory over a stubborn enemy, while the enormous significance of the event was more clearly understood abroad than within Russia itself. The establishment of Russian sovereignty on the Caucasian isthmus has so many consequences, both definite and probable, direct and indirect, that it is still impossible to grasp them all; they will reveal themselves, one by one, in such a long chain of events that only the next generation will know the full scope of the events of 1859.

It is not yet possible to write a history of Russian dominion in the Caucasus. For the history of such a long and complex period, it is essential to study the materials that have been piling up in the archives for sixty years; a special commission has only recently undertaken this task. One day Russia will read the complete history of the Caucasian War, which is one of the greatest and most captivating episodes in our history, not only because of the significance of the issues resolved by Russian arms in this isolated corner of the empire, but also because of the extraordinary exertion of the human spirit that marked the struggle on both sides; because of the unprecedented persistence with which it persisted for decades, continuously changing its character; and because of the unique moral character, if one may say, of those soldiers who were relocated to the Caucasus. It is wrong to embark on such a study with only a partial understanding, but it is possible to illustrate the significance of the Caucasian War in its causes, progression, and results. That is the aim of this book. Every Russian should know, at least in the most basic sense, what is being done in the Caucasus, where two hundred thousand of his countrymen are fighting.

The beginning of the Caucasian War coincided with the first years of the current century, when Russia brought the Georgian Kingdom under its rule. This development defined the new attitude of the state toward the half-wild tribes of the Caucasus; once foreign and alien, they became domestic. Now Russia had to subordinate them to its authority. Thus arose a long and bloody struggle which remains unfinished to this day. The Caucasus demanded great sacrifices; yet, whatever the cost, no Russian has the right to complain, because the occupation of the Caucasian regions was neither an accidental nor an arbitrary event in Russian history. It had been centuries in the making, prompted by the great needs of the state; a prophecy which fulfilled itself. As early as the sixteenth century, when the Russian people developed in solitude on the banks of the Oka and Volkhov rivers, separated from the Caucasus by a vast wilderness, sacred duties and great aspirations drew the attention of the first tsars to this region. The domestic struggle with Islam, which had been pressing Russia from all sides, had been resolved. Through the ruins of the Tatar kingdoms that had been founded on Russian soil, a vast horizon to the south and east opened to the Muscovite state; there, in the distance, were free seas, abundant commerce, and like-minded peoples—Georgians and Caucasian highlanders, then still half-Christians, who extended their hand to Russia. On one side the Volga led the Russians to the Caspian Sea, surrounded by wealthy nations who had not a single boat between them—to a sea without a master; dominance on this sea was necessary to secure dominion over the weak and fragmented territories of the Pre-Caspian Caucasus. European trade, seeking access to the golden countries of the East, tried to force its way through the Muscovite state and its neighboring deserts, and carried the Russians along on the road already indicated by the natural position of their land.

On the other side, the groans of Orthodox Georgia, trampled by barbarian invasions and exhausted by endless struggle—fighting at that time not for the right to be an independent nation, but only for the right not to deny Christ—reached Russian ears. Islamic brutality, fueled by the new doctrine of Shi'ism, was in full swing.[1] Desperate to overcome the steadfastness of Christian tribes, the Persians systematically slaughtered the populations of entire regions. Since the sixteenth century, almost every Georgian family could pray to the martyrs of their own blood. One after another, Georgian shrines were brought to Moscow to preserve them from desecration by the Muslims. Tsar and commoner alike listened with equal sorrow to the stories of infidel violence committed against the Orthodox population of Georgia; the people's deepest sentiments were affected, pulling the Russians to the path already indicated by politics and trade. Indeed, from the sixteenth century onward, the Russian tsars began their attempts to simultaneously support deteriorating Georgia and to assert their commercial and political dominance in the Caspian countries. These attempts continued, ever increasing in scale, until the end

---

[1] Although Shia Islam was by this time nearly a thousand years old, having formed in the immediate aftermath of Muhammad's death, it was newly ascendant in the sixteenth century; at the dawn of the century, the Safavids took power in Persia, and converted the Persian people away from their traditional Sunni faith, establishing the first major Shia state in history.

of the eighteenth century.

At first, the obstacles appeared to be almost insurmountable. Russia did not yet border the Caucasus; between them lay a vast desert, filled with roaming predators and gangs of reckless daredevils, almost impassable. But in the meantime, the Russian people grew, communities spread out, and the desert gradually gave way to settlements. At the beginning of the eighteenth century, the whole area from the Oka to the mouth of the Don, and from Kazan to Astrakhan, was occupied by a chain of villages and towns. From that time, a series of Caucasian campaigns began under Peter the Great, Catherine I, Anna Ivanovna, Catherine the Great, and Paul I; they became more and more frequent as Russia advanced toward the Caucasus. By the end of the century, the Russian people had reached the European frontiers of their land—the Black Sea and the foothills of the Caucasus. The Transcaucasian territories were no longer in such a remote geographical position in relation to Russia as Khiva is now; Peter the Great's plans could be carried out without the difficulties they encountered in 1722.

At the same time, a new pogrom and renewed violence on the part of the Muslims befell Georgia. Now, standing on the Terek and Kuban rivers, Russia could no longer confine itself to fruitless lamentations, as it had in the sixteenth century, while listening to stories of Persians forcing Orthodox Christians to spit on the miraculous image of the Virgin Mary on the Kursk bridge in Tiflis, throwing the disobedient (and all were disobedient) into the Kura river, soon dammed with bodies; or hearing how two thousand worshipers from the David Gareja monastery were brought under the axe during the observance of Matins on Palm Sunday. Aside from the most significant interests, wherein the possession of the Caucasus was already a matter of paramount importance for the empire, the religious matter meant that Russia could not refuse to defend Orthodox Georgia without ceasing to be Russia. With the Manifesto of January 18th, 1801, Paul I accepted Georgia as a Russian province in accordance with the will of the last Georgian king, George XII.

At that time, only Turkey disputed Russian supremacy on the Black Sea. However, Turkey had already been declared politically insolvent; she was under the care of Europe, which jealously guarded her integrity, because she could not take an equal part in the dispute alone. In spite of this artificial equilibrium which teetered on the point of a needle, a struggle began between the two great powers for the dominant influence over Turkey and all that belonged to her. Europe was penetrating the backward mass of Asia from two sides, from the west and south; for some European nations, Asiatic concerns were of paramount and exceptional importance. Within Turkey's diplomatically assumed—if not actual—domain lay the Black Sea and Transcaucasia; this state extended its claims to the shores of the Caspian Sea and could easily enforce them on the basis of its first success over the Persians. But the vaguely delineated mass of the Turkish empire was already beginning to drift from one influence to another. It was evident that the dispute over the Black Sea, over all the waters and lands over which the Turkish claims extended, would sooner or later, at the first convenient political opportunity, become a European dispute and be turned against us, because questions of Western influence in Asia do not tolerate partition; a rival there is a mortal threat to European power. Whichever influence or dominion extended over these countries (among which were lands which had no masters, such as the whole of the Caucasian isthmus), it would become hostile to us. Meanwhile, dominion over the Black and Caspian seas, or at the very least the neutrality of these seas, is a vital question for the whole southern half of Russia, from the Oka River to the Crimea, where the principal forces of the empire, both personal and material, are becoming increasingly concentrated. One could say that this half of the state is created by the Black Sea. Before Catherine's conquest, it was in the same position as the Ural region and southern

Siberia: a settlement pushed into the impassable steppe; possession of the coast made it an independent, wealthy part of the empire. In a few years, with the construction of the Transcaucasus Railway (which will necessarily attract to itself vast trade with the Trebizond Empire of upper Asia), with the rapid development of the Volga and sea shipping, and with the establishment of Asian trade, the desolate Caspian Sea will create for southeastern Russia the same conditions that the Black Sea has already created for southwestern Russia. However, Russia can only protect its southern basins from the Caucasian isthmus; a continental state like ours can neither maintain its importance nor make its will respected where its cannons cannot reach by solid ground. If Russia's horizon were closed to the south by the snowy peaks of the Caucasus range, the entire western mainland of Asia would be completely beyond our influence and, given the present impotence of Turkey and Persia, would not have to wait long for a master or masters. If this has not happened or will not happen, it is only because the Russian army, standing on the Caucasian isthmus, can embrace the southern shores of these seas, stretching its arms in both directions.

The hostile influence would not stop at the Caucasian isthmus. A series of water basins pushed deep into the Asian mainland—from the Dardanelles to the Aral Sea—with its navigable tributary, the Amu Darya, cutting across Central Asia almost to the Indian border, is too tempting a route for the trade now making its way across the roadless ridges and high plains of Armenia and Azerbaijan. European trade with Asia had been conducted along this route for thousands of years; interrupted by the Turks when they took Constantinople and sealed the Black Sea, trade would have been resumed at the beginning of this century if the Caucasian isthmus had remained without a ruler. But who does not know the true nature of European trade in Asia? The coming together of two such unequal powers begins with chintzes and ends with the creation of a subject empire of 150 million inhabitants. If some European trade had established itself in the interior Asiatic basins, before or in addition to our dominion over the Caucasus, its path would have defined the limit of our relations with Asia. Everything lying beyond the line stretching from the mouth of the Kuban to the northern shore of the Aral Sea would have merged into one group hostile to us, and our only gain would have been that the entire southern frontier of the empire, for several thousand kilometers from the Crimea to China, would have become a frontier in the full sense of the word, requiring fortresses and an army for its protection. The defense of the Caucasian line would probably require the same troops that now occupy it, but without any hope of ending this situation. European trade with Persia and inland Asia, passing through the Caucasian isthmus, subordinate to Russian control, promises positive benefits to the state; the same trade, passing through the Caucasus independent of us, would create for Russia an endless series of losses and threats. The Caucasian army holds in its hands the key to the East; this is so well known to our adversaries that during the past war it was impossible to open an English pamphlet without finding therein talk of a means of cleansing the Transcaucasus of the Russians. While the relations to the East are a matter of the highest importance for others, for Russia they fulfill a historical necessity that we are powerless to evade.

Russia, covering a territory of ten thousand kilometers, does not touch but mingles with Muslim and pagan Asia. Its borders are pushed forward not by political calculations alone, but also by the demands of internal management and the domestic economy, like the cultivated fields of an owner who has settled in a new land that belongs to no one. Beyond the Russian frontier, all the way to the ends of the earth, everything in Asia smolders and collapses. Asiatic societies held on for centuries, like a corpse untouched by air in the grave, preserved by the absence of foreign elements; as soon as the living forces of Europe breathed on them, they began to crumble. The present peoples of the western half of Asia have long ceased to be social organisms; they have become a mass of Muslims, randomly united, without the slightest sympathy, under this or that local authority. Islam penetrated into all their social pores and completely displaced nationality, as lime mortar displaces little by little all the substance of an ancient shell, taking its form; it took possession of the whole man and fossilized him, leaving no room for either social or personal development which does not arise from the Quran. The civil organization of Muslim nations, their courts, finances, personal, and family relations are established by the Sharia as an immutable revelation, unchangeable to the end of time. Even more than the society, the personality of man is sedated in Islam. In this respect Islam may well be called a rational religion; it explains the world and gives man a purpose in a rational, natural way, quite close to the universal tradition, intelligible to every mind and therefore perfectly satisfactory; but at the same time, it is presented without the slightest moral ideal that could sanctify the soul. Islam takes human nature as it is, with all its virtue and all its filth, blesses everything in it equally, gives a legal outcome to good and bad, and promises the continuation of such a state for all eternity. The duties imposed by this religion consist of simple ritualism and a hatred of infidels. The Muslim derives from his faith sufficient intellectual satisfaction and unperturbed contentment with himself. This attitude can only result in extreme apathy. What can a man aspire to when he is already all that he ought to be, a man who is neither gnawed by doubt nor beckoned by any ideal? Islam has swept over the earth in a fiery torrent and is now producing terrible fires in the places where it is penetrating anew, as exemplified by the Caucasus. The first explosion of Islam derived its power precisely from the sanctification of the evil aspects of human nature—unbridled passions, beastliness, and fanaticism.

In essence, Islam is a religion of passion, a truly

incendiary doctrine; it inflames people, doubles their strength, and makes them capable of great things to the extent that there is enough fuel in a person or a nation. When the spiritual fire burns out, all that will be left of Islam is ashes, barren rituals, social and mental stagnation, and the apathy of a hungover drunkard. In three centuries, Islam exhausted its shallow content entirely and has been frozen like a corpse ever since. Whoever has seen and knows the Asiatic peoples of today—whoever knows to what extent they are strangers to the notion of fatherland, to any public interest, to the first duties of a citizen; to what extent they are indifferent to that which people call their land, as long as their personal peace is not disturbed; to what extent they despise their governments, without even thinking of improving them; how little they are moved by domestic events—cannot for a moment doubt that the final hour has struck for these assemblages of men devoid of any inner connection. The efforts of some Muslim governments to reform the state to European standards have destroyed the last foundation of these decrepit peoples: faith. The social law of all Muslims, the Sharia, is a revelation; to destroy or change it is to reject the word of God.

The reforms in Asia have, on the one hand, alienated the masses, led them to ferment, and created a Muslim freemasonry very similar to Muridism at its beginning, which covered most of the Muslim world with secret lodges; on the other hand, they have created an official class of educated Muslims who place their faith in money alone, no matter who it is that's giving it to them. What will happen to Asia cannot yet be predicted, but it cannot continue to exist in the form it does now. Either it will undergo an internal upheaval, of which there is no sign, or it will become prey. In any case, Russia cannot allow the fate of a large part of the world, with which it is almost indivisibly linked—with which it lives, one might say, under the same roof—to be decided without its participation. The solution of the dispute between Christianity and Islam, which had been abandoned by

Europe since the fourteenth century, has since that time, as if by divine will, been left to Russia alone and has become, consciously or unconsciously, her people's business. All her sympathies and all her interests, even independent of her will, from century to century, periodically put her face to face against every possible variation of this question.

The real link between Russia and Asia, their node, is in the Caucasus. In the rest of the territory between settled Asia and the Russian frontier, from the Amur to the Caspian Sea, stretches a desert, which may become somewhat populated and passable by the end of the century; but much can happen before then. Through the Caucasian isthmus and its basin, the Caspian Sea, Russia is in direct contact with the whole bulk of Muslim Asia. From the Caucasus, Russia can reach everywhere she needs to go; and it is here that the half-century-long struggle against Islamic fanaticism created the only army that can endure, without breakdown, the endless hardships of Asiatic campaigns.

For Russia, the Caucasian isthmus is a bridge from the Russian coast to the heart of the Asian continent, a wall to protect Central Asia from hostile influences, and an advanced fortification protecting both the Black and Caspian seas. The occupation of this region was the first necessity of the state. But while the Russian nation reached the foot of the Caucasus, everything changed in the mountains. Knocked out of European Russia, Islam worked tirelessly for three centuries to strengthen the natural fence of Asia and the Muslim world—the Caucasus range—and achieved its goal. In place of the Christian tribes of old, we met in the mountains the most ferocious embodiment of Muslim fanaticism. For sixty years the storming of this gigantic fortress continued; all the energy of ancient Islam, which had long ago left the relaxed Asiatic world, was concentrated at its edge in the Caucasian mountains. The struggle was furious, the sacrifices terrible. Russia did not lag behind but overcame, knowing that great nations, on the way to their appointed goal, encounter obstacles equal to their strength.

MURIDISM

In the spring of 1801, General Knorring brought Georgia under Russian rule. At this time all the countries of the Caucasus, both the mountains and the countryside, were in a state of perfect chaos; society was disintegrating not from internal decay, but from endless external violence. The whole Caucasus had been turned into a slave market. It is enough to remember that the entire armies of the Mamluks and the Baghdad Gurjas were composed of Caucasian slaves; that the original Janissaries were of the same origin; that all the white slaves of Turkey and Persia were exported from the Caucasus; and that the Turkish harems were filled with Caucasian women, causing the ethnological change of the Ottoman horde into the present Turkish one; combining all these factors, one can imagine the situation from which Russia extracted the Caucasus. Since the Georgian kingdom, which had once ruled over the mountains, was trampled by the invasion of Genghis Khan's horde, any idea of law and order disappeared from the Caucasian isthmus. The local tribes became divided into two parties, hunters and prey, depending on whether they lived in impassable slums or in open fields. But even this distinction disappeared over time. Accustomed from childhood to catching people, the mountaineers became so familiar with this craft that they transferred it to their own canyons. Returning from hunting in a foreign land, they set a trap for a neighbor, stole his children, and sometimes sold their own. Cargoes of slaves were sent from the Caucasus by land and sea; not Blacks, as on the Guinea coast, but people of European origin, mostly Christians. In the full swing of the eighteenth century, the Caucasus lived the life of prehistoric times, as when the foundation of world slavery was laid for ancient societies by the same means.

When Georgia came under Russian rule, this disgrace came to an end—but not overnight. In order to rid the Transcaucasus of Lezgin gangs, it was necessary to exterminate them over a period of fifteen years, as one exterminates beasts of prey; however, the Russian forces in the mountains at the time were not large, and they were engaged in a more pressing struggle. Persia and Turkey, separated for three centuries by irreconcilable enmity, rose in unison against Christian rule in the Caucasus; our troops had to wage a long and persistent war, outnumbered ten to one. Fortunately, at that time the Muslim states had already outlived their glory days and retained only the appearance of their former power; the first encounter with Europeans exposed their impotence. Nevertheless, the numerical forces of Persia and Turkey were so great, their efforts to knock us out of the Caucasus so persistent, that the small Georgian corps had to concentrate almost all of its forces on the southern border; few battalions remained to protect the Transcaucasian regions from the mountaineers, and they had no hope of carrying the war into the mountains, limited by necessity to the pursuit of bandit gangs inside the region. The offensive war against the mountaineers only really began with the appointment of General Yermolov as chief administrator of the Caucasian region in 1816.

At that time, the entire mountain belt of the Caucasian

isthmus, from the Black Sea to the Caspian Sea in length and from the Kuban and Terek to the southern slope of the range in width, was occupied by independent tribes hostile to us. Only two roads connected the Transcaucasian regions with Russia: one was the Darial, laid from time immemorial along the Terek gorge through the middle of the Caucasus range, and the other along the Caspian coast. Both could be passed only by columns ready to repel the enemy at any moment. The inhabitants of the mountains, irrespective of the fundamental differences between the tribes in external appearance and language, have always been imbued with the exact same attitude toward whatever neighbors they had: the character of people who have become so familiar with predation that it has passed into their blood and created of them a predatory breed, almost in the zoological sense of the word. For thousands of years the Caucasian mountaineers had borrowed nothing from their neighbors except innovations in weaponry—a matter in which they were highly adoptive; in all other respects there was no intellectual contact between them and their neighbors. Caucasian societies have preserved in their bottomless gorges the primitive image of tribes whose traces have long since disappeared from the earth, just as remnants of antiquity are preserved in graves. They were separated from the inhabitants of the foothills not only by mountain ranges, but also by the succession of centuries that had passed since their separation from the human family. The mountain tribes did not communicate with the people of the foothills or with their mountain neighbors, and little by little each tribe lost the feeling of its blood unity, breaking up into small societies limited by the space of one mountain valley. Here was the mountaineer's only fatherland, the only corner of the earth in which he recognized man's right to live; he looked at the rest of the world with hostility and considered it legitimate prey. Now philology alone can reconstruct the historical character of the tribes that settled the Caucasus, can link them to something that exists or once existed. The tattered ribs of the Caucasus bear the traces of all migrations of the White race, historic and prehistoric, like the wool of driven herds on a barbed fence. These fragments are buried in inaccessible gorges, petrified in their original form, and now represent a collection of living samples from an epoch of which nothing but a few incomprehensible legends remain. But while science has not yet touched the subject, we know plainly that the Caucasus range is inhabited by seven entirely different peoples. Dagestan, submissive and unruly, is occupied by three tribes, which the Russians have christened by the common name of Lezgin, but which differ radically in language and outward appearance. The first tribe, the Tsunta, lives along the mountain ridge facing Georgia; the second, the Avar, is settled in the northern part of highland Dagestan; the third, the Gazikumukh, occupies the country east of these tribes to the Caspian Sea. On the northern slope of the mountain range—which cuts the eastern Caucasus diagonally from southwest to northeast—lives a Chechen tribe that calls itself the Nakh. The middle ridge of the Caucasus, the narrowest and highest, is inhabited by the Ossetians (Alans), a tribe of comparatively recent origin, because some (albeit faint) trace of their migration to the Caucasus still flickers in history. The entire western group of the Caucasus is occupied by the numerous Adyghe, commonly called Circassians, who also settled the Kabardian plain in later centuries. Finally, in the corner between the western ridge, the Black Sea, and Mingrelia, the Abkhaz tribe was founded.

In olden times, the population of the mountains, consisting of these seven primitive peoples, stretched quite far in all directions across the surrounding plains; they were trapped in the gorges of the Caucasus by the invasion of Genghis Khan's Tatar horde, constituting the last tribal influx on the Caucasian isthmus. The Tatars had occupied the foothill countries on three sides and in the middle of the Caucasus range, between the Ossetians and the Adyghes, cutting into the depths of the mountains and exterminating the natives. However, in some of the wildest and most inaccessible valleys of the Caucasus, on some terraces which rose, isolated, among the chaos of rocks and spurs, fragments of tribes survived in a handful of villages, inhabited by people who spoke a language understood by no one; such exceptions are quite numerous. The differences between the tribes of the Caucasus consist not only in their languages, but also in their outward appearance; the spiritual makeup of the people is also quite distinct and proves that these tribes have broken away from their roots to vastly varying degrees of development. The powerful Adyghe people represent a social state strikingly similar to the barbaric life of the fifth and sixth centuries, grounded in recognized laws and therefore containing the germs of development that would be possible if this people were located in a different position; at the same time, the majority of the Lezgins of the Dagestan highlands and the Chechens form a type of society so disintegrated that there remains nothing but individuals who tolerate each other purely for fear of blood feuds. The influence of Islam, which had established itself in coastal Dagestan under the Abbasids, imposed on the eastern Lezgin tribes a certain tinge of civil organization, if only by subjecting them to hereditary rulers who could cut the heads off their subjects with impunity. Christian enlightenment of the southern mountain tribes of Tsunta and Ossetia, which was undertaken during the golden age of the Georgian kingdom, disappeared together with the influence of Georgia, leaving no traces in the former tribe and only vague memories in the latter. The rest of the mountain population, especially in the eastern part of the Caucasus, remained inaccessible to outside influence for millennia. Locked in their impregnable gorges, the Caucasian mountaineers went to the plain only to plunder and slaughter; at home their days passed in the dullest idleness. Nowadays, a mountaineer of any means sits motionless from morning till evening in the doorway of a shack, carving a stick with a knife.

Religion, if there had been any religion other than sham-
anism among the eastern Caucasian tribes until recently,
had long since been forgotten, leaving no trace of thought
of a higher world, no shadow of a notion of any duty, nothing but fear of certain impure influences. Without hope,
without responsibility, and without thought—without a fatherland except the few houses of his village—living by robbery and without fear of any retribution for it in his sheltered nest, spending thus century after century, the Caucasian mountaineer has cultivated in himself the nature of a
carnivorous beast which lies senselessly in the sun until it
feels hunger and then torments its victim without malice or
remorse. Since the thirteenth century, the Caucasus developed an industry of hunting people for sale, which reduced
the mountaineer's conception of life to the final degree of
defilement; he began to understand the worth of a human
being only in the amount of silver for which he could be
exchanged. With all this, it should be noted that the corrup-
tion of the Caucasian tribes was only external. The mountaineer was like a child brought up with bad examples, who
adopted them unaccountably but still retained all the fresh-
ness of his dormant soul; he never fell to the degree of the
Guinean Negro, retaining over him the immeasurable advantages of his pure, richly endowed Japhetic lineage. The
unspoiled nature of these people is evident in the fervor and
devotion which Muridism—the first general idea that penetrated their thought—kindled within them. All the energy
that the mountaineers had developed over centuries of
combat, they now devoted to this new religion. Until that
point, they had been warriors for the sake of war—brigands
or mercenary soldiers. The only armies in the East which
were capable of opposing the Europeans—after the waning
of the first explosion of Islam—were always composed of
Caucasians; pure Asiatic armies could never withstand the
European onslaught except by disproportionate numerical
superiority. It is ridiculous to compare the Caucasian mountaineers with the Algerian Arabs or Kabyle people, whom

French rhetoric has made out to be fearsome opponents. At no point could any number of Algerians take a blockhouse defended by twenty-five soldiers. Adyghes and Lezgins have taken fortresses defended by an entire Caucasian battalion with their bare hands; they have marched against the bayonets of intrepid soldiers who were determined to fight to the last man, who blew up powder magazines at the last stand, and still they went; they piled the ditch and covered the bulwark with their bodies, blew up in the air alongside the defenders, but took possession of the fortress.

In the 1780s, banditry in the defenseless foothills was the main trade of the mountaineers. What agreements were possible with such a people, divided into hundreds of independent societies? During the first period of Russian rule in Georgia, when the Caucasian authorities demanded that the Kura Khanate—comparatively the most educated group among the Lezgins—suppress their robbers, Kura elders answered: we are honest people, we do not like to plow land, we live and will live by robbery, as our fathers and grandfathers lived. By what means, besides arms, could the mountain tribes be restrained? Meanwhile, these tribes separated the Transcaucasian regions from Russia by a continuous belt between two hundred and two hundred fifty kilometers wide, leaving Russia no means of communication with its new possessions other than through this hostile region. To possess Transcaucasia, it was necessary to conquer the Caucasus.

The execution of such a task was incomparably easier in the beginning than it is now. At that time, the unruly mountains consisted of one eastern group; the western Caucasus still nominally belonged to Turkey and was sufficiently guarded by the Black Sea and Linear Cossacks who lived on the frontier line without disturbing our forces. In the 1820s, there was no political connection between the mountain societies and sympathies were seldom manifested. When there was a case of a raid into our borders, the daredevils from different tribes flocked under the command of a prominent mountain ataman and then went home. This was an organization of private individuals in which societies played no part. There was no loot in sight, and there was no alliance. That is why, during our advance, each society defended itself and was subdued separately. Muslim fanaticism did not yet exist among the highlanders, nor did the religion itself, except for the name, and therefore their conscience was not troubled when they recognized the power of infidels. Defending their independence, the highlanders defended only the right to plunder the foothills. Lastly, the power of ordinary weapons against a people who had seen nothing of the kind was at first overwhelming. In the 1820s the highlanders could not withstand artillery fire; in spite of their bravery and agility, they were powerless before a closed mass, as before a mobile fortress. The bravest brigands do not quickly and easily turn into warriors. In this state of affairs a detachment of a few companies could be considered self-sufficient in the Caucasus and could act offensively against a divided, indifferent, disorganized enemy. There was only one difficulty: the endless fragmentation of the military theater into separate cells, each requiring an independent operation. No matter how weak the enemy's resistance may be, in such a cluttered area as the Caucasus it was impossible to make a sudden jump across several cells. In order to move from one conquered valley to the next, navigating a barely passable mountain range in the process, it is necessary to occupy the first one firmly, to transfer to it the very foundation of the forthcoming expedition, otherwise the campaign would be only a raid; and what results can be expected from a raid in a country where one has to climb a mountain all day long, stopping every minute to catch one's breath? In the Caucasus, to move forward meant—and means—to move gradually, firmly occupying each valley, which requires one of two things: either great strength or great time. Under the first assumption, we could act unceasingly, advancing on all sides from the circumference to the center; under the second assumption, we had to wait for the newly conquered societies to get accustomed to our power, to turn into obedient tributaries, and only then, without fearing for our rear, to undertake further conquest. In that era it was preferable to rely on time. Back then nothing yet foretold the future explosion; it was reasonable to think that, however slow our operations might be, we would succeed in subduing the highlanders before they changed their ingrained customs. Meanwhile, maintaining troops in the Caucasus cost twice as much as in Russia. On this basis the Caucasus Corps was left in its original strength, even though hundreds of thousands of Russian soldiers had returned from abroad. Forty-five thousand men were required to act offensively and defensively at the same time against a hostile country one thousand kilometers long, encircling it from both sides. Under such conditions, action on our part could not be decisive despite the fragmentation of the enemy.

General Yermolov did not have enough forces to conduct several operations at once, and was forced to restrict himself to those that were most essential. For all that, much was accomplished during this period, which has remained in the memory of Russia not without reason. The occupation of the Shakhmal domain, the conquest of the khanates of Kura and Gazikumukh, of Akusha, of Great and Lesser Kabarda, and the pogrom of Chechnya connected the Transcaucasian regions with Russia by two broad belts of subjugated countries, cut the hostile region into two separate groups without communication, and greatly shook the mountaineers' confidence in the impregnability of their refuges. Another ten or fifteen years of similar efforts, against a similar enemy, would probably have accomplished our desired goal. The eastern Caucasus, surrounded by our possessions, absorbing the greatest part of our force, would have been subdued. But we ran out of time. As soon as the Persian and Turkish wars diverted the Russian forces to the southern border, the religious conspiracy, which had been secretly undermining the ground beneath our feet for several years, suddenly threw off its mask and drew the entire population of the mountains into a ruthless battle against the Christians. The position of Russian rule in the Caucasus suddenly changed.

It will probably be a while before anyone counts up the millions of rubles and thousands of people that the appearance of Muridism in the mountains cost Russia. The impact of this event has been far reaching, much farther than it may seem at first sight. In any case, it is important for the state—both in the past and in the future—to try to define its thought.

Islam entered the Caucasus from two directions. The eastern mountains received it from the Arab Caliphate in the seventh and eighth centuries, the western mountains from Turkey in the seventeenth and eighteenth centuries. The depth of the roots that Islam spread in the Caucasus corresponds to the relative antiquity of these epochs: in the eastern half it penetrated the majority of the population, in the western half only the upper class. This fact explains why the Lezgins were so soon attracted to Muridism and why the Adyghes, despite all the efforts of Murid preachers, were so reluctant to succumb to it. But even in the eastern group, not all tribes were equally bound to Islam. For a long time Islam in this region was confined to seaside Dagestan alone, checked in the mountains by the influence of Christian Georgia. It was only with the fall of the Georgian kingdom that the mountain societies began little by little to become accustomed to the rites of Islam, though it was still far from being equally prevalent when Muridic preaching began in the Caucasus. The preaching immediately attracted the old Muslims of coastal Dagestan, but in the mountains it triumphed only after a serious struggle. Up to that time, Islam had been widespread in the Caucasus for centuries without influencing the social or personal condition of the mountaineers; everything that has been said about the pagan tribes applied equally to the Muslim tribes, the only difference being their shaved heads. The highlanders succumbed to Islam because it justified their ferocious character and gave it a legitimate sanctification. Sharia preached personal revenge at home, jihad against neighbors, and indulgence of the passions; it did not disturb tranquility of conscience with ideals, comforting the highlanders with the promise of a tempting paradise, and all this for the observance of a few insignificant rites. Its noisy appearance in the world, which had innumerable tangible consequences, had no influence on the spiritual side of man, nor did it bring a single new impulse into the life of the peoples who submitted to it.

When Europeans observed the African tribes who had embraced Islam, they were struck by the fundamental impotence of that religion on moral character; nothing distinguished the Negro Muslims from the faithless Negroes, except the turbans on the heads of significant individuals. It cannot be otherwise. Islam, depending on whether the circumstances are more or less favorable to it, either eradicates the nationality altogether, leaving in its place one numerical collection of units, or remains an external ceremony without any relation to life. Uncivilized pagans who have embraced Islam say "God" instead of "gods," perform five ablutions a day, and continue to live as before. The Quran inspires in them only unperturbed self-satisfaction, fanatical hatred of everything non-Muslim, apathy under ordinary circumstances, and jittery enthusiasm at the eruption of fanaticism. With all this, in the first, weakest degree of development, as soon as the Muslim begins to reflect, he can no longer look at the world with the eyes of a pagan pantheist. He sees in nature something quite different from the law of senseless necessity, under the authority of which man so indifferently spends his life in half-awake reverie. Illumined by the idea of one God, Creator and Provider, the Muslim does not regard himself as a minute manifestation of eternal power, he recognizes his free personality and feels a natural longing for a higher standard. But, turning to religion to satisfy this first need of the awakened soul, he finds in it only barren dogmatism, without love and without a moral ideal. It is difficult for man to reconcile himself to such a position. For centuries, the best men of the Muslim world have tried to discover in their theology an answer to the voice of conscience; they have produced many interpretations which have no theological difference, but differ in their answers to the fundamental question of how man should understand his duties to God. Longing for a more sincere relationship with the Creator than merely the fulfillment of material rites, and having failed to find love in their law, the zealous Muslim teachers involuntarily replace it with zeal—intense hatred of non-believers and fanatical exaggeration of all the tenets of the faith. Muridism is the latest historical phenomenon of this kind, the most exaggerated of all.

Attempts have been made to connect the origin of Muridism with the Ismaili and Hashshashin sects; its appearance in the Caucasus was attributed to Bukhara. There may be a basis to this, but it is not necessary to explain this doctrine. Muridism could have been born in the Caucasus, as various Muslim currents are now born in Asia, from a natural need of the spirit awakened but not satisfied by the Quran; it developed to such extent because it served as an expression of the main focus and feature of Islam—hatred of infidels—in a country occupied by infidels. Muridism did not create its own theology; it differs from the faith common to all Sunnis only in the extremity of its conclusions. Its preaching is based on a special explanation of the tariqat, the part of the law containing the doctrine of the duties of man. Yet in this respect, it has surpassed every degree of Muslim atrocity and may be thought to have spoken the final word on Islam. Muridism has cut off all humanity from man's life and has set him two rules: a minute-by-minute preparation for eternity and a continuous war against the infidels, giving him the choice of death or observance of these rules in all their fanatical rigor. The Sharia was restored to its primitive form. An unconditional standard was placed over people and any distinction between them was determined only by their spiritual status. The advocates of Muridism took the shortest way to their goal and, without waiting for the feeling of religious equality to become a habit, preferred to establish it with an axe. The rulers, nobles (where they existed), hereditary chiefs, people of respected clans—or simply respected personally before the advent of Muridism—were slaughtered one after another, and for a time perfect equality really settled down in the mountains, because there was no one left but commoners. For a bride, whether she was the daughter of the foremost chief or the lowliest shepherd, the price was invariably set at 1 ruble. Everything that resembled the past—dances, games, playing the balalaika—was declared a secular rite worthy of death. Unconditional obedience to the senior clergy, as in a monastery, became the primary duty. Fanaticism and fear changed the people, who until then had recognized nothing but personal discretion.

The sacrifice of property, life, and family—when the power demanded it, of course—counted for little. Aspiring to enslave people entirely, mind and soul, Muridism had to subordinate them to its immediate supervision. In all the mountains, homes were assigned to the supervision of Murids, before whom even the secrets of the Asiatic terem were opened; they were responsible for every action, for the whole domestic life of the people subordinated to them. The strict observance of even the most trifling rites of faith was, of course, the first law of the new doctrine, but it was not content with this. Playing with the will and habits of people, Muridism forbade something new every day: today smoking tobacco, common to all Muslims; tomorrow using garlic, without which a mountaineer could not live; and so on. Corporal punishment was forcibly introduced among people who used to consider it a shame if someone had been flogged as a child. By subordinating human life in its entirety, by converting, or at least striving to convert, its followers into blind instruments of what it called the will of God, Muridism surrounded itself with sworn proponents—

Murids, people who surrendered to it with their eyes closed, swearing an oath to fight to the last breath and to slaughter anyone who was pointed out to them, no matter who he was, whether friend or father. These men became the initiated brothers of the spiritual order, the shepherds of the human flock subjugated by Muridism; they alone held power and honor. Finally, at the head of this monstrous society stood the imam, the mediator between God and the believers. The Murids understood the title of imam in its original meaning, in the sense of the heir of the prophet, inspired from above, penetrating all the seven meanings of the Quran, placed over the earth to fulfill the word of God. Every order given by the authority was therefore endowed with the character of infallibility, and every transgressor was an enemy of God. The ultimate consequence of Muridism was the destruction of the idea of personal responsibility in man. Everyone was given an external law, the exact fulfillment of which would lead to salvation; everyone was assigned a teacher who was responsible for ensuring that he fulfilled the law and was saved, willingly or unwillingly. Muridism stripped life naked and in return for all that it had deprived man of, filled his soul with the follies of Islamic mysticism. By this means it formed a political society of several hundred thousand people, until then unprecedented in the region, who placed both will and conscience in the hands of the authorities. If not literally, then at least in its main features, Muridism realized this ideal and immediately turned the brotherhood it created into a war machine against us.

The population of the mountains was reborn. Seizing control of everyone and everything, Muridism replaced the scarcity of its means with energy; in the wild mountains, which for thousands of years had rejected any civil organization, it created a public treasury, provision stores, gunpowder factories, artillery, and fortresses. Instead of isolated, disorganized communities, we were met in the mountains by a solid mass that repelled every blow with a common effort. When our troops entered the lands of any community, the inhabitants willingly and unwillingly left their homes and provisions as sacrifice and hid in the slums, wherein every step on our part resulted in enormous losses. The women and children, deprived of daily sustenance, were placed in neighboring villages and somehow sustained until the next harvest; the men, like a pack of hungry wolves, rushed into our borders and lived by plunder. Those who starved to death, as well as those who fell in war, were regarded as martyrs who had attained their life's purpose. Peaceful and non-peaceful societies alike were infected with the teachings of the corrective tariqat. The difference between them was only in the relative impregnability of the places they inhabited; by this alone they measured their relationship to the Russians. Invariably, the first appearance of the Murids served as a signal for an uprising among the subdued tribes. A peaceful village, just passed by a Russian column, could sometimes turn into an enemy position within an hour. Wherever a Russian detachment stood, its rear was never secure. Suddenly rushing from one direction or another, the Murids continually kindled fires in the region and forced our columns to abandon what they had begun to run back and defend places for which they had never before feared. The mountaineers, carried away by fanaticism, spared no thought for tomorrow, unhesitating as they left their ancestral homes and young children to go fight the Russians. Even now, driving through Dagestan, one sees everywhere stone carcasses of villages of the most durable, centuries-old construction, completely empty. Their inhabitants were at Shamil's disposal; they abandoned the homes of their forefathers, their life of freedom, to huddle on bare cliffs, to live with whatever God sent them, all to meet the infidels with weapons in their hands. The fire of fanaticism eventually began to cool, but for fifteen years the Caucasian land was literally burning under Russian feet. Muridism, like a wild beast, was gnawing at its cage, trying to break free. If Russian force had not encircled it with an iron girdle, one can be sure that it would have spilled over

Muslim Asia in an unstoppable stream and would now be striving for the realization of the second caliphate. The mere title of imam, adopted by the chiefs of the Murids, sufficiently shows where the new doctrine was aiming.

Muridism, in all its evolving nuances, was embodied by the four men who took turns in leading its destiny. The first was the creator of the new doctrine, Mullah Muhammed al-Yaragi, the Qadi of Kyurin. He created the notion and system of Muridism, completely finalized, with all its implications. In his rural school, in the village of Yarag-Kazmalyar, in the midst of the Russian possessions, the idea of a future struggle was born and matured; from there it was spread by preaching throughout Dagestan. In 1828, in a small garden which can still be visited, a few mullahs, disciples of Muhammed, held the last council at which it was laid down to reinstill Islam and drive the Russians out of the Caucasus. The consequences are notorious. Mullah Muhammed was the soul of Muridism, but he himself never took the stage, never received superiors, never even preached publicly. He only created the doctrine and prepared the people. All the leaders of Muridism came out of his school.

The banner of gazavat, the war of faith, was raised by his most beloved disciple, Qazi Mullah, and the whole of coastal Dagestan was dragged behind him. Qazi Mullah was a shallow theologian and an unsophisticated politician, but he possessed a quality that utterly captivated the masses—passionate conviction. When he spoke in a popular assembly or addressed the army during a battle, the crowds obeyed him as one man, living only by his will. Even now, the mountaineers who remember Qazi Mullah say: "The heart of a man stuck to his lips: with one breath he awakened a storm in the soul." Having rushed into an open fight with the Russians in the first fever of fanaticism, Muridism raised everything to the ground, withstood many bloody battles, forced us to strain our strength, but was finally knocked down from the coastal country and driven into the mountains, where few tribes still sympathized with it. Qazi

Mullah perished in the rubble at Gimry.

For a few years Muridism disappeared from sight as if it had never existed at all; it was forgotten. But during this time, it was alive and at work. Driven from the field, it settled in the mountains inaccessible to us, and there, by seduction and war, by treason and open force, united little by little all the mountain tribes under one spiritual authority. At that time its leader was Gamzat-bek, a man who seemed to be specially created for such a role. For Muridism, the time of passionate enthusiasm and open struggle had passed. For the time being, it had to act through underground channels, little by little, day by day. Gamzat-bek, pious, silent, and ruthless—who thought deeply about his enterprises and executed them quickly and without publicity, "for God and not for himself," as he put it—achieved his goal in three years, establishing Muridism in the mountains on the corpses of friends and foes; it was all the same to him. It was during this period that the best people in the mountains were slaughtered in order to establish universal equality. When Gamzat-bek died under the blows of murderers avenging their blood, Muridism was already in possession of the mountains and could fight again under a new leader: Shamil, also a disciple of Muhammed al-Yaragi.

Having established itself in the mountains, Muridism ceased to be a religious party. It formed itself a state on its own model, and Shamil, the first of the leaders of this doctrine, united in his person the power of a spiritual leader and a people's ruler. He truly attained the height of this position, merging the mountaineers into one social body, creating means not seen before him, realizing the political ideal of Muridism—monstrous, of course, but true to its goal. Consolidating gradually, as the habit of obedience took root in the mountains and fanaticism cooled down, Shamil's power took the shape of ordinary Asiatic despotism. Yet, in the first period of his reign, Shamil was an imam, a religious leader, more than any of his predecessors; it was at this time that the bloodiest struggle raged against Muridism—which was spreading unstoppably in all directions—until at last it came to the point that in 1843 Chechnya was wrested from our hands, our fragmented and weak troops were driven from the field into Dagestan, and the 5th Infantry Corps had to move from the Dniester to the Caucasus, to recover the lost cause.

The first explosion of Muridism surprised but did not puzzle the Caucasian authorities. It was a revolt of the subjugated Muslim population, an unexpected but ever-possible event, and therefore quite understandable. Initially, the revolt had ample opportunity because most of our troops were far away, deep in Asian Turkey. However, after the conclusion of peace, sufficient forces moved into Dagestan and the revolt of the seaside region was suppressed by two campaigns in 1831 and 1832. It was then that Muridism hid in the unruly mountains and we lost sight of it. Considering everything to be over, we did not pay any attention to the internal quarrels of Lezgin tribes, quarrels by which Muridism ultimately subjugated the whole of mountainous Dagestan in a few years. The acquisition of the western mountains, completed previously according to the Treaty of Adrianople, diverted the main attention of the Caucasian authorities to that direction. The submission of the eastern shore of the Black Sea to Russian rule was undoubtedly an extremely important event, placing the whole Caucasian isthmus under our absolute power; moreover, since the treaty was only a document which the Adyghe tribes did not care to recognize, it was possible to force them into submission with weapons alone. For the next six years, from 1832 to 1839, the main forces of the Caucasus Corps, which had been operating in the eastern Caucasus up to that time, were exclusively directed against the western mountains, the Kuban, and the Black Sea. In Chechnya and Dagestan there remained an insignificant number of troops under the control of local chiefs, deprived of any autonomy. Nowadays one cannot fail to see that such a sudden change of course was a great mistake. Of course the empire must at all costs conquer the whole Caucasus, but conquest of the western mountains was not the first nor the most urgent task in the Caucasian War. The Adyghes live in a corner of the country that makes up the Caucasian viceroyalty. On one side they are surrounded by the Russian population of the Caucasian line, on the other by the Georgian population of Imereti and Mingrelia, who are firmly loyal to us. No matter how brave the mountaineers are, they cannot overpower a regular army in an open battle and take possession of any part of the region by force. Their invasions are dangerous to us only where they draw the fanatical native population after them, pitting our weapons against the innumerable obstacles of folk warfare. The unruly tribes of the western Caucasus, though numerous and brave, can do nothing of the kind when surrounded by Christian nations, and by the very nature of things are hopelessly imprisoned in their own land, lying in a corner of the Caucasus far from all our communications. By contrast, the unruly tribes of the eastern Caucasus were extremely dangerous to us. The only two land connections between Russia and the Transcaucasus, the Darial gorge and the Caspian coast, run at the very foot of the eastern group of mountains, encircling it, so that the slightest success of the enemy in one direction or another would cut off the path connecting the state with its country regions. The eastern group of the Caucasus lies in the middle of the Muslim section of the viceroyalty, which naturally sympathize with their fellow believers. It was in these mountains that the banner of gazavat, the war of faith, had just been raised; from there, the call went out for all Muslims to stand up against the rule of the infidels. Such a situation, dangerous in peacetime, could become disastrous in an Asiatic conflict; meeting the enemy ahead, our troops could be suddenly cut off from the rear. The rebellion produced by Muridism was suppressed in the Caspian region, but it was known that the remnants of it had taken refuge in Lezgistan.

After the example of 1831, prudence demanded that we

pursue the conquest of the eastern mountains, still divided into small societies, more persistently than ever before, and not slacken in our efforts until completion. The western Caucasus would have had its turn. But at that time we were carried away by the news of acquisition and obsessed with the idea that it was necessary to isolate this part of the dominions, which had not yet been conquered, from the Black Sea; the untenability of this idea was only fully apparent in 1854. In the course of six years of action against the western mountains, Muridism, which appeared in Lezgistan as an exile but was not persecuted on our part, grew into a terrible force and conquered the whole country. Our occupation of Avaria, after the Murids had exterminated the line of Avar khans who were subject to Russia, brought us face to face with Muridism again. This region—pushed into the heart of the mountains and exposed to attack from all sides—had to be protected from enemies. The military actions of 1837 and 1838, undertaken with the local means of the Dagestan detachment, revealed the strength which Muridism had acquired through our negligence, and in 1839 forced us again to transfer the main operations from the western Caucasus to the eastern. But the situation was already irreparable. General Grabbe took Shamil's residence after the bloody siege of Akhoulgo, exterminating the majority of mountain youths who flocked under the imam's banners and forcing Shamil himself to flee to the other side of the mountains, to Shatoy; but Muridism had managed to take root in the people's minds to such an extent that a few months after Shamil's defeat, Chechnya, which had been neutral up to that time, rebelled against us and recognized the power of the imam. Muridism had taken possession of the whole eastern cluster of the Caucasus and turned its forces to the war against the infidels. There was no hope of suppressing it in the mountains except by conquering the mountains themselves. Yet for this it would have been necessary to change the whole system of warfare. We were no longer dealing with unconnected societies, resisting or conquering separately, but with a state, extremely militant and fanatical, submissive to an authority vested with infallibility, and possessing several tens of thousands of soldiers protected by a terrible terrain; a state, in addition, surrounded by tribes sympathetic to it, ready to take up arms at every success of their religious kinsmen and to put our troops between two flames.

It is obvious that in this state of affairs no invasion of the mountains, undertaken in the sense of a European campaign, could succeed, no matter what forces were used for that purpose. The aim of such an invasion is to break the armed forces of the enemy, to seize the main centers of his land and, having made it impossible for him to continue resistance, to force him to accept our terms. In the Caucasus mountains the armed forces are all the inhabitants, from twelve years of age to the utmost decrepitude. There are no population centers there. In Chechnya the inhabitants are scattered in small hamlets throughout the dense forests. In Dagestan there are quite a few large villages, but they are all fortresses; the majority of the population lives there in small settlements, a few houses with towers clustered like bird's nests on the ribs of cliffs and mountain ledges. A Chechen village had to be reached through a thicket occupied by the enemy, agile and fast as forest beasts, paying a soldier's wages for every step of the way. The Dagestani aul had to be taken by storm, climbing up a steep path, under a hail of bullets and stones thrown from the cliffs. Near a Chechen settlement was another settlement, near a mountain aul another aul, with which the same thing had to be repeated. Here and there only the walls were left in our grasp, because the inhabitants always managed to escape. It was necessary to feed the army from its own confines, limiting the duration of the campaign to the provisions taken, or to send a column after it, with the danger that it would be exterminated because the route traveled closed behind the detachment like the trail of a boat in the water. The residents, knowing that the whole purpose of the campaign was ruin, fought bitterly for their property. It is clear that under such a system of defense, no army could be raised to destroy all Chechen villages and Dagestani auls, even if it were more numerous than that of Batu. No mountain society could surrender separately to avoid ruin, even if it wanted to; the combined forces of Muridism would crush it. In order to make any part of the mountains recognize our authority, it was necessary to open the region with unhindered communications, to make it accessible at any time of the year, to protect the native population with troops, returning to those troops the natural advantages of regular weapons by destroying those obstacles that protected the enemy. In a word, the war had to become methodical, to defeat nature, and to subjugate people for as long as it was necessary to complete our work unhindered.

It goes without saying that it would have been impossible for even the largest army to advance in this manner, from the circumference to the center, developing the terrain in all directions. The eastern group of mountains, dominated by Muridism at the time, is about nine hundred kilometers in circumference. All this mountainous space is so cluttered with ridges, torn by ravines, and clothed with a half-impenetrable forest, such that even on a relief map it is a perfect chaos in which the eye can hardly grasp the main outlines. It would take half a century, if not longer, and the sacrifice of half a million soldiers to make the whole country accessible, ridge by ridge, gorge by gorge, overcoming at every step the fierce resistance of the mountaineers. But in spite of its chaotic appearance, this military theater has, like any other, its strategic lines, the possession of which decides the possession of the known part of the region. The ridges, accessible only in summer, cut the region into practically independent sections; the rivers, cutting through the bottomless abysses of the Caucasus, form lines of the strongest defense. Even the tribal divisions in the mountains form edges as sharp as the natural features, the mutual dislike of the tribes restrained but not erased by Muridism; edges that could serve as stages of conquest. Strategic lines existed, but to discern them in such a cluttered terrain alone required the eye of a commander the likes of whom had not appeared in the Caucasus for a long time; to approach them properly required a perfect knowledge of local warfare. However, if in the course of eighteen years—from the time when the main effort was again directed against the eastern Caucasus to the final three years of the operation—no first-class military man capable of conquering the mountains had appeared in the Caucasian army, there were certainly intelligent and extremely experienced generals who could march toward this goal, slowly but surely, and hold back the further onslaught of Muridism. But here is the main drawback of man's power—a full understanding of the present belongs only to the minds of the first-rate, which are few in the world; the range of ideas of ordinary people, though intelligent, as well as of the masses, is not really determined by the present, but by the period immediately preceding it, which has already had time to articulate, agree on its concepts and impregnate the general opinion with them. If in the current period something new is formed and develops quickly, intelligent people still approach it with old methods and constantly lag behind the actual state of things. This is exactly what happened in the Caucasus.

After Muridism had subjugated the population of the eastern mountains and transformed them into a militant Muslim order, the commanders stationed in the Caucasus did not want to realize for a long time that twenty years of work toward the conquest of this country were gone, that it was necessary to forget about them and start work again as if we had just arrived in the region; that it was impossible not only to act the way General Yermolov did, but even the way General Rosen had acted against the disunited mountaineers in 1832 now that they had merged into one political whole; that now individual societies could not submit to a pogrom even if they wanted to; that the land of unruly mountaineers had to be torn off piece by piece; that the army must establish itself in the occupied area. Considerable forces are necessary for methodical warfare, yet at that time they squandered eighteen battalions for the Black Sea coast line, which had to be abandoned at the first enemy shot, they allocated means to make strong expeditions beyond the Kuban, which was not the most urgent demand of the Caucasian War, and even in Chechnya and Dagestan they collected detachments of ten and twelve battalions of the same strength as the detachments which have now conquered the Caucasus. Behind these detachments there were not so many reserves as now, it is true, but this lack of reserves was a reason to act more slowly, not a reason to act incorrectly. Unfortunately, the memories of the previous period still weighed too heavily on the decisions of the Caucasus commanders. It was also difficult to admit that the enormous sacrifices made for the conquest of the area had been wasted and that it was necessary to start again. Without admitting it, they redoubled the ferocity of their assault on the mountaineers in order to correct the mistakes of many years at once. The main blows were directed at Shamil personally—at his residences and his promoters, hoping to overthrow Muridism and break his power over the highlanders. But Muridism was no longer a party; it was a state. Our troops met unanimous resistance everywhere. For several years, expeditions to Chechnya, Ichkeria, and the countries surrounding Avaria were tirelessly carried out with the aim of forcing the mountain societies to break away from Shamil by ruining their lands. Sometimes the troops penetrated far enough into the enemy's country, sometimes they encountered insurmountable obstacles from the first steps, but always these expeditions had the same result: a few burnt out huts, costing us several hundred, sometimes several thousand, soldiers. Our offensive was incessant but largely innocuous for the highlanders, who were so emboldened by this that a few dozen men, huddled in their slums, were not afraid to engage a column of several battalions and, answering with one shot to a hundred of ours, inflicted a much greater loss on us than we did on them. During these years it happened more than once that the mountaineers, relying on the fortification of their land, rushed into our borders as we were advancing on them, disturbing the submissive population and sometimes established themselves in the areas occupied by them. Muridism expanded its stranglehold slowly but constantly, driving us step by step out of the eastern Caucasus.

To put an end to this miserable state of affairs, Prince Chernyshov, the former Minister of War, was sent to the Caucasus in 1842. Unfamiliar with the situation of the country, he could not replace one system with another and, in order to stop the constant failures, he stopped military operations altogether. Muridism was given a year's rest, during which it settled in definitively. In 1843, the mountaineers themselves rushed from the depths of their gorges, took Avaria and Koysubu from us—despite the fact that the population of these countries bravely supported our cause—exterminated several detachments, took nine fortifications, and spilled over the whole of Dagestan, where only two sites remained in our grip: Temir-Khan-Shurá and Nisovoyeh. Although the Caucasian Corps had been constantly reinforced since 1831 by increasing the number of battalions in the regiments and forming forty-seven new line battalions, in the spring of 1844 we had to move another forty thousand bayonet troops to the Caucasus. This year our troops operated not as detachments, but as an entire corps; and yet, strange as it may seem to say, superior morale remained on the side of the mountaineers. The troops were well aware of their superiority, but the commanders were afraid to make up their minds on decisive actions, constantly expecting some extraordinary and crushing maneuver from the Murids—the incidents of the two preceding years had made them so accustomed to this threat. The events of the Caucasian War had subverted the most plausible expectations to such an extent that at last even experienced men began to consider it an absolutely extraordinary phenomenon, beyond all rules and calculations.

However, the main hazard to Russian rule on the Caucasian isthmus was not so much the insurmountable terrain of the mountains as it was the disposition of the tribes surrounding them. If the force hostile to us had been limited to independent mountaineers, this danger could have been mathematically calculated and sufficient means could always have been used to counter it. But, as has already been said, the only difference between the submissive and disobedient Muslim tribes was the relative fortitude of their lands; by this alone did they measure their attitude toward us. Every invasion of the Murids was followed by an uprising of the peaceful people, so that in the event of an external war it was impossible to calculate the extent of the conflagration which might break out at our rear. Every tribe around the Murids not only sympathized with them, but was directed to lend them a hand at the first opportunity. In this respect, the administration of the region was even more flawed than the manner of warfare itself.

In Islam, every aspect of the people's public and private life, every relationship, is determined by Sharia; thus, in a purely Muslim context, any legislation becomes impossible: a law is already established by the unchangeable will of God, and all people, perfectly equal among themselves, are equally obliged to obey it. In practice, there are many violations of this fundamental law in Muslim lands, but the rule is invariable, and Muridism, having subjected everything to the spiritual law without question, has only brought to completion the doctrine common to all Muslims. The interpreters of the law must naturally be the clergy who learn it; hence the introduction of Sharia law into a country gives full authority to the clergy. It is needless to say that in the Caucasus the Muslim clergy was secretly devoted to Muridism. This doctrine fulfilled their most intimate convictions and desires. The clergy had no influence under the former tribal system. Mountain and sub-mountain tribes were subordinate either to the rulers, the upper class, or the people's assembly; but, in general, they were governed according to the ancient custom, sometimes in a very complicated and harmonious way. In the 1820s, the authorities created by the folk communities were eliminated and the rule of the Sharia began to spread. The Caucasian authorities and Shamil and his followers were equally eager for this. Muridism exerted all efforts to exterminate local rulers and upper classes, to eradicate ancient folk customs that divided and distinguished tribes, replacing them with the rule of Sharia and clergy everywhere. The Russian authorities in the Caucasus did the same in the subjugated societies, for a very comprehensible reason: it was easier for them to base the people's government on the Sharia, the written law, than on unknown tribal customs, which had yet to be clarified and legitimized at a time when there were not even properly organized local authorities in the Caucasus. It was according to this system that Russian hands cultivated the soil on which Muridism was later sown. The teachings of the strict tariqat were spread throughout the Caucasus by persons on the Russian payroll. What could be expected from the population, armed and ignorant, to whom the most incendiary ideas were preached daily while they saw with their own eyes the impotence of Russian arms against Muridism? Naturally, the whole population of the foothills was waiting for any opportunity, and Muridism could nourish the most fantastic hopes.

Under these difficult circumstances, the chief command in the Caucasus was entrusted to the late Prince M. S. Vorontsov, who was vested with full authority. The constant failures of the previous campaigns were attributed not to a false system, but to inexperienced commanders. Relying on the high-profile fame of Prince Vorontsov, decisive successes were expected from the moment he set foot in the Caucasus. Prince Vorontsov's initial military venture, the Dargo Campaign, was planned under the influence of these expectations and was executed on the model of previous expeditions, only on a larger scale; this was also the last venture of its kind. The lesson was sufficient. A campaign undertaken into the mountains with a numerous and superior army, supplied with all possible means, and inspired by the personal leadership of a famous and authorized general, ended with the loss of five thousand men and three guns, without the slightest gain. From this point on, a change took place in the Caucasian War. It cannot be said that Prince Vorontsov replaced the former puzzling expeditions with a coherent system fully applicable to the present situation. During his administration, the offensive was systematically carried out in only one corner of the military theatre: on the Chechen plain. There, for the first time under Muridism, a positive result was achieved; by well-considered and steadily executed felling of the forests, the hostile population was driven out of lesser Chechnya and the development of Greater Chechnya began. In other parts of the enemy's land—in Dagestan, the Vladikavkaz district, and on the Lezgin line—expeditions were still tentative, attempts made without a firmly defined goal. It is impossible to say, even with the greatest desire, that the sieges of Gergebil, Saltov, and Chokha, or the campaigns to Dzhurmut and Kapucha, were links in any greater system or steps that would move us in a positive direction. All this aside, the course of action undertaken by Prince Vorontsov was imbued with one common idea and did in fact bring about a beneficial change in the Caucasian War.

The principal feature of this course of action was that we temporarily abandoned the conquest of the mountains, which we had so persistently and vainly sought before, without, however, refusing take advantage of circumstances wherever possible. We began to conduct our expeditions cautiously, not far from our borders, without exposing the active troops to great danger. The Caucasian Corps, reinforced on the departure of the Fifth Infantry Corps by a new division of twenty battalions, became tighter around the mountains because the troops were no longer diverted to the far ends of the region or deep into the enemy's land; the unruly mountaineers saw an iron wall encircling them, and thus the victories and the spread of Muridism were put to an end, which was the great merit of Prince Vorontsov.

Of course, more could have been done in ten years. Yet, carried away by old memories once again, by fear of the extraordinary successes the Murids had achieved in the past, we let our concerns overtake us and became desperate to break the mountaineers right away. We took fortresses at a high price, losing a whole summer and several thousand soldiers for the siege, and then abandoned them; meanwhile, half of the detachment used for the siege could have defeated the mountaineers without loss, if they had thought of invading our borders. Again, reason was guided by our understanding of the preceding period, not the current one. Nevertheless, the close ten-year imposition had its effect on the recalcitrant mountaineers. Although the hostile disposition of the mountain population was by no means weakened, because the incendiary rule of the Sharia and the influence of the clergy had meanwhile been definitively systematized, fanaticism had lost some of its vague hopes, which constituted half of its strength.

The rebels, locked up hopelessly in their mountains, could no longer think of driving us from the Caucasus by their own forces, and their fervor cooled. The force of Muridism seeped away. Its champions became significant people and took the place of the aristocracy which they had slaughtered in the 1830s. Shamil, growing accustomed to the position of an Asiatic sultan, forced the mountain societies to recognize his son as heir and considered founding a ruling house. Desperate ventures no longer attracted the aging knights of Muridism. The people, at first devoted with all their souls to the new doctrine, became cold to it when they experienced in practice the monstrous despotism of the government, which had once been promised to them as the ideal of earthly life. The passion passed away little by little, but it was replaced by habit and the extraordinary development of political power based on Muridism. The material resources of the mountaineers increased enormously—they already had excellent fortresses, gunpowder factories, foundries—replacing the fervor of the fanatical crowd with a social and military system. The eastern Caucasus, like Proteus, changed its appearance every decade, remaining equally invulnerable to our weapons.

By the end of Prince Vorontsov's administration, military operations were taking place exclusively on the Chechen plain, where the current commander-in-chief, Prince Baryatinsky, was in charge. There we were moving forward, gradually opening up Greater Chechnya by siftings; it was also here that we laid the foundation for a reasonable management of the native population, based on tribal identity, with the elimination, where possible, of the spiritual element. But the actions of the commander of the left flank were limited, both by the insufficiency of means and the subordinate nature of his position. For the rest of the hostile frontiers the troops stood, one might say, gun at their feet, not daring to act, but so too not daring to weaken themselves by a single company, so as not to give Muridism any breathing room. The idea of conquering the mountains, at first postponed indefinitely, began to disappear altogether, even in the minds of people who had devoted their lives to war in the Caucasus. By the beginning of the 1850s, the very few people who believed in the possibility of defeating Muridism surprised, but did not convince anyone, with their words. The fifty-year struggle on the Caucasian isthmus led to the empire chaining the whole army to the eastern group of mountains, removing it not only from Russia's total forces, but even from the number of mobile forces in the Caucasus, with no foreseeable conclusion ahead.

In 1853 an external war broke out. Up to that time the struggle against Muridism had taken place in the midst of a profound peace, which enabled the empire to dispose of its forces freely. Then, for the first time, the question which had long troubled farsighted men became a reality: what would be our position when the Caucasian Corps would have to withstand the onslaught of external forces in the internal war that had assumed such enormous proportions. This question was solved by the prowess of the Caucasian troops, who several times defeated armies four or five times stronger than any regular army. However, during the three-year war, the fate of Russian rule in the Caucasus frequently hung in the balance. The Caucasian troops had to face both sides, meeting the enemy from north and south, in the midst of a population awaiting the first success of their co-religionists. The obsolete leaders of Muridism did not do anything decisive at this time, though they could have, and probably would have, if our defensive lines on their side had been weakened. Overconfidence could have been our undoing; one need only remember 1843. Although the Caucasian troops were reinforced during the war by four divisions and their number expanded to 270,000 armed men—capable, with their superior quality, of breaking any European enemy—the necessity of containing the internal enemy absorbed all the forces of the Caucasian Corps to such an extent that on the battlefields of Turkey, the fate of the war was decided by nine battalions in 1853 and seventeen battalions in 1854. These detachments had to fight in a ratio of one against five, and to win at all costs, because with Muridism in the rear there was no retreat; even an unresolved affair would have all the consequences of a total defeat for us. The troops which operated on the Caucasian frontier from 1853 to 1855 were strong in spirit and confidence, but so weak in numbers that even a small increase of the enemy, an easy feat for the allied army, would invariably have tipped the scales in the allies' favor. Now, after the fall of Shamil, we can say frankly that in spite of a number of truly unparalleled feats, we retained the Caucasus only because France—which possessed the dominant land forces in the previous war—was alien to the Asiatic question and had no interest in dislodging us from the Caucasus; furthermore, when the British army was increased in 1856 to such a size that it could begin independent action, the sudden peace put an end to its enterprises. Given the situation that Muridism created for us in the Caucasus, it was more than doubtful that in 1855 or 1856, out of the 270,000 armed men that made up the Caucasian Corps, it would be possible to safely separate forces sufficient to repel a 50,000-strong European landing. In the winter of 1855–1856, over a period of three months, they could not muster enough troops to give battle to Omer Pasha, who had invaded Mingrelia with 25,000 Turks.

The war had made clear the position of Russian power in the Caucasus, as well as many other things in the empire. After such an example it was no longer possible to consider the Caucasian struggle as a local affair, the influence of which extended only to one corner of the Russian possessions. In fact, it turned out that this struggle robbed the state of half of the active force it could have had at its disposal for foreign warfare. Of the 270,000 troops that were immovably chained to the Caucasus from 1854 to 1856, the defense of the Caucasus from external enemies, including all garrisons of frontier fortresses, numbered hardly 70,000; the remaining 200,000 were a fruitless sacrifice, cut off from the state by Muridism. With the high cost of sustaining troops in the Caucasus, these 200,000 were equal to at least 300,000 in Russia, i.e., almost the whole mass of our active forces, consisting of the guards, grenadiers, reserve cavalry, and six army corps. Moreover, these 200,000 soldiers and Cossacks were not militia or reserve battalions, of which any number could be recruited so long as they serve only for the internal defense of the region; they were first-rate soldiers, the very element that we lacked in the Crimean War and which the Allies had in 20,000 Algerian soldiers, deciding everything. The absence of such a mass of select troops from the war theater reduced the actual strength of the Russian Empire to that of a state not with 70 million, but with 30 million inhabitants. What was the ultimate result of this immense sacrifice? That 270,000 troops were insufficient for the defense of the Caucasus in an external war, as long as armed Muridism stood in the middle of it.

After such an experience, there could be no more hesitation. The Russian Empire could not abandon the Caucasus without giving up half of its history, both past and future; therefore, it had to take advantage of the peace to subdue the mountaineers as soon as possible. The necessity of the immediate conquest of the mountains was realized, but this realization did not make the task itself any easier. The Caucasian War consumed so many troops, it passed through so many systems that were satisfactory on paper but turned out to be completely untenable in practice, that there was no room for doubt. To end the war, it was not mere manpower or military plans, no matter how well drawn up, that was necessary; it was a commander. All that remained was to find him.

CONQUEST OF THE CAUCASUS

With the end of the international war, the tsar elected Adjutant General Prince A. I. Baryatinsky, who had been prepared for this position by his long and active service in the Caucasus, as commander-in-chief of the separate Caucasian Corps. In addition to the forces of the Caucasian Corps (after some time rebranded as an army), the Thirteenth and Eighteenth Infantry Divisions were left at the disposal of the new commander-in-chief, along with three newly formed dragoon regiments. Since 1856, the government had maintained a constant supply of forces and material means in the Caucasus sufficient for the persistent conduct of the war.

The Caucasian army and the Caucasian population accepted the appointment of Prince Baryatinsky with unanimous joy. Anyone who was then in the Caucasus will not forget the kind of festivity which erupted all over the country as the news spread. The general feeling is quite understandable in this case; the appointment of Prince Baryatinsky was a natural appointment, which the whole Caucasus desired and expected. The peculiarity of this country, so different from other parts of the empire, as well as the exceptional character of the troops occupying it and trained in it, have long manifested themselves as harshness and independence, which one must fully understand to rule wisely in the Caucasus. God alone knows all the consequences that occurred from the introduction of ideas *a priori* into the management of the Caucasus and the conduct of the Caucasian War by people who needed to learn on the job. Irrespective of Prince Baryatinsky's personality, which had long been highly esteemed, the Caucasus trusted him as its own man, who knew both people and matters and could take up the task directly. His appointment as commander-in-chief made a deep impression on the troops, on the people, and on the unruly mountains. The newspaper *Kavkaz* was filled with joyful reviews from all parts of the country. Among other things, it reported: "Two hundred thousand Caucasian soldiers consider the appointment of Prince Baryatinsky as a reward for their service." Abandoned in a land quite unlike the rest of Russia, placed in exceptional circumstances, they had to forge a peculiar personality; yet no man will regret the experience, when the personality he forms has the following features: that a Caucasian soldier in the tsar's service does not consider death or victory as the last degree of a warrior's energy; that he will swear to his commander to win and fulfill his oath at least against an enemy four times stronger than himself, because he does not consider anyone stronger than himself as long as a weapon is in his hands. But the more developed and the more peculiar the personality of a Caucasian soldier, the more important it is for him to be under the hand of a superior who understands him. That is why, when the news of the appointment of Prince Baryatinsky as commander of our corps spread, old servicemen at all ends of the Caucasus told their young comrades: "Look, a prayer to God and service to the tsar are never wasted." At the same time, for the first time since the beginning of the mountain war, the imam of Muridism, alarmed by the general popular apprehension, sent out an announcement to the tribes that the Russians were going to conquer all the mountains in two years and that the time had come when every true Muslim must lay down his life for the faith. This is not at all what the mountaineers thought when the former commanders-in-chief were appointed—or, better to say, they did not think about it at all, caring little, in the midst of their strongholds, who was in charge of the Russians. Life experience often confirms that great events are in fact foretold by a shadow that looms ahead of them, which the masses, always gifted with a marvelous instinct, already feel, while the most advanced people are yet to notice anything. Such was the case when Prince Baryatinsky was appointed commander-in-chief. Until then the idea of conquering the mountains had only glimmered as a possibility in the indefinitely distant future. When the new commander-in-chief took charge, the troops marched on with the idea that they were now making not one of countless expeditions, but beginning the conquest of the mountains; meanwhile, an anxious expectation of decisive events spread among the unruly population. I do not know why such a general mood took possession of the region—the military fame of Prince Baryatinsky was not then sufficiently established to inspire such confidence—but it was so.

Simultaneously with his appointment, Prince Baryatinsky requested a new division of military commands in the Caucasus. Until then, they existed in the same form as they were established before Muridism, meeting the needs of a completely different era, when the purpose of military action was only to protect our borders or punish independent predatory societies. Since then, the tribes of the eastern Caucasus had merged into one political body, and the enemy, surrounded by a network of small commanders, had become stronger than each of the military leaders opposing him, so that the opposite was the case: unity on the enemy's side and fragmentation on ours. Embarking on decisive action, it was necessary to entrust power to an independent commander in each independent military theater. In August 1856, five commanders of troops were established according to the natural division of the Caucasus, vested with the rights of corps commanders. There were two against the Adyghes of the western Caucasus: the commander of the right flank on the northern side of the mountains, and the governor-general of Kutaisi on the southern side. Against the Murids of the eastern group, there were three: one on the northern slope—the commander of the left flank, to whom Chechnya (former left flank), the Vladikavkaz district, and Kabardia (former center) were subordinated; another in Dagestan, to whom the whole Caspian region was entrusted; and the third on the Lezgin line, on the southern side of the mountains, facing Georgia. This division was involuntary. Each of the designated large divisions was delineated by nature itself, having its own sharply different climatic and local conditions, and in front of itself a different enemy and a separate military theater, which local troops had to develop before embarking on collective actions.

The commander-in-chief could not conduct operations himself when they were of a local character; he had to leave the execution of his plan to his assistants, success hinging on their talent and energies. The choice of corps commanders for the Caucasian theater was even more difficult than for the European, because their actions would be more independent; the personality of the men was in this case a matter of special importance. The first assistant to the commander-in-chief was, of course, the chief of the army's main staff. Prince Baryatinsky invited General Milyutin to this post, who, although he had not yet occupied any high office, had already acquired general fame as an excellent officer, as a writer, and as a creator of military statistics, which he had elevated to the rank of a science for the first time. Besides the extremely difficult position of chief of the main staff of such a motley army as the Caucasian army, General Milyutin was also entrusted with bringing into line the new military administration of the Caucasus, of which only the general features had been outlined by the establishment of troop commanders. In terms of military administration, it was possible to recount almost all the years of Russian rule in the Caucasus by the various institutions that existed, each expressing the character and needs of a different era. General Milyutin developed a new system of military administration with such completeness and structure that it will remain a monument to the present Caucasian leadership for a long time. The new administrative system—which has not yet been completed in all its elements due to the vastness of the work—has already grasped the main issues, laid the foundation for reasonable management of the mountaineers and, by distributing the institutions according to the actual needs of the region, begun to replace the former unity of arbitrary bureaucracy, which had been spread over the most diverse country in the world, with a living, adaptable organization. The foundation and example for the new system was the management of the Chechen people arranged by Prince Baryatinsky when he was chief of the left flank—a system already justified by experience. The accomplishment of this truly statesmanlike work, in which General Milyutin was the only assistant to the commander-in-chief, could not be slowed down either by campaigns or by his countless other occupations. General Milyutin's labors and actions earned him a rare position: the universal respect of the army and the region, without the slightest shade of opinion.

According to the commander-in-chief's plan, the most extensive and difficult military operations were to be undertaken by the commander of the left flank troops. General (now Adjutant General and Count) Yevdokimov was appointed to this post, together with the new division of the Caucasus. The forested Chechnya was a classic land of failure, not to say defeat, experienced at the hands of the mountaineers, but conquest was to begin here; our troops were to penetrate deep into this land at a time when Muridism still stood at its full strength. Under these conditions the plan of the commander-in-chief could only succeed with a perfectly faultless execution. The local terrain was everywhere the terrain of the Ichkerian and Dargin expeditions—one awkward step would have led to the same results—and a considerable failure on our part, only one, would have again postponed the conquest of the mountains for an indefinite time. Count Yevdokimov executed the plans of the commander-in-chief with rare perfection. It can be said positively that not once during the three-year war did he allow the highlanders to engage us where they wanted or where it could be beneficial for them. When undertaking the riskiest ventures, Count Yevdokimov always managed to solve the matter with clever maneuvers, calmly finishing the proposed work and forcing the mountain hordes to disperse without a fight, which more than anything lowered the morale of the enemy. His system of action, in which not the bayonet but the axe was the main instrument of conquest, by necessity burdened the troops with excessive labor and caused them the same loss from disease as they had previously suffered from fire, but the psychological effect of this loss is quite different. When the head is taken off, one does not weep for the hair, and the Caucasus was now subdued.

The former Pre-Caspian commander, Adjutant General Prince Orbeliani, an experienced general who enjoyed the confidence and love of the troops, was left in charge. A year later Prince Orbeliani received another appointment and surrendered his post to Adjutant General Baron Wrangel, who was to finish the work of Count Yevdokimov and, in his final campaign under the personal leadership of the commander-in-chief, to inflict fatal blows to Muridism. The command of the Lezgin line was appointed to the brave Baron Vrevsky, who laid down his life in this war, and taken over on his death by the young but experienced General Prince Melikov. I limit this overview of commanders to the subject of this work: the eastern Caucasus. The selection and distribution of the chief commanders, perfectly adapted to the nature of their actions, ensured the precise execution of the commander-in-chief's plan.

The main effort was directed against the eastern mountains, for reasons already stated. This part of the Caucasus cut off our rear, constantly threatening communications, and at the same time served as a fortress for Muridism, providing a base from which it could stir the obedient Muslim population into constant agitation. The eastern mountains constituted the main danger and the main obstacle to Russian rule on the Caucasian isthmus. Prince Baryatinsky left a limited force in the western Caucasus, sufficient to gradually develop access to the mountains and perform all preparatory work by the time the war in the eastern Caucasus reached its conclusion. Then all available forces were moved against the latter.

The plan for the conquest of the eastern Caucasus, conceived by Prince Baryatinsky long before his appointment as commander-in-chief, was executed in three years, word for word and line for line, as, perhaps, a military plan has never been executed before. The wisdom of his foresight, self-evident to those who have read his letters or reports from the years prior, will stand the test of time. This plan was similar to a proper siege of a fortress, but on a much greater scale, connecting all the preceding systems in due time. The chief defense of the mountaineers was not in the middle of their land, but along its circumference. The frontier line was like a bastion, which we were forced to approach openly as they sheltered behind powerful barriers; the fortresses of the Murids stood on the frontier line, housing a population of hardened warriors, educated by constant warfare and shaped by half a century of struggle into our personal enemies. Most of these obstacles did not exist in the depths of the mountains. Once in the heart of the mountains, local obstacles were equal for the enemy and for us; there were no prearranged means of defense there; the population, distant from us and never disturbed, was much less belligerent, much less imbued with hatred toward us, and valued their well-being more than the semi-nomadic

Abreks of the frontier societies. Our main objective was to make a secure path into the midst of the mountains. The first condition for the success of such an enterprise was choosing the best route. Then what remained was to act as in a siege: firmly occupy the incoming roads to the mountains, move forward methodically, dislodge the obstacles hindering us on both sides, stand firmly at select points in the mountains themselves, and then proceed to a rapid offensive with the whole mass of troops, fracturing the enemy's country from the core and forcing the frontier line to fall without resistance. Obviously, according to the very essence of this program, the conquest was to pass through three phases: the preparatory period for occupying the proper approaches, a period of methodical warfare in the mountains and, finally, the decisive offensive.

This comparison with the siege of a fortress expresses only the general principle of the plan. The outcome depended on correctly selecting the points of interest and operational lines that would decide the success of the enterprise quickly and completely. Until then, determining the goal of operations had been a stumbling block in the Caucasian War. It constantly turned out that occupation of the points considered decisive was of no use and we abandoned them ourselves. In such a congested terrain as that of the Caucasus, this choice is extremely difficult—but in it the skill of the commander is revealed.

Ever since Muridism united all the eastern tribes into one nation, the mountain societies had become parts of a single organism that felt all blows received equally, no matter from which side they were dealt; tribal identity had already half-melted into political unity. Subjected to a common authority, moving in crowds from one part of the region to another to protect their borders, and forced to exchange products exclusively among themselves because the foothill region was closed to them, the highlanders in some manner became citizens of one state. In such a state of social order, the conquest of significant tribes from one side was bound to reverberate throughout the mountains and shake the courage and confidence of the entire population. The conquest of Dagestan would decide the fate of Chechnya, and vice versa. Thus, the choice of a path for the offensive depended primarily on the relative ease with which the second part of the operation—methodical warfare in the mountains—could be accomplished.

On the southern side, the unruly population was fenced in by a snowy ridge, where the passes thaw for only three months in the summer. During the rest of the year, it was impossible for a mass of troops to cross this ridge. When attacking from the southern side, it was necessary to leave the troops without communication for nine months of the year in the midst of a hostile population. Only quick invasions in summer were possible on the Lezgin line. Expeditions of this kind, as had already been proven long ago, could not conquer the mountaineers; their troops covered the foothills with familiar ease, advancing on the enemy and gradually exhausting him before the time came for decisive blows. The only choice left for a real offensive was between Dagestan and Chechnya.

Decades of expeditions within the borders of unruly Dagestan, from Akhulgo to Chokh, proved the futility of such attempts. Every village in this country was a Saragossa. We were taking a fortified aul at the cost of several thousand sacrifices, only to discover a number of similar aulas requiring the same sacrifices. Dagestan was a nest of Muridism. The spiritual power slavishly subjugated the Dagestani population, mastered the thought and will of its people, and reigned over them unquestioningly. It was impossible to hope to shake the political power of Muridism in this country while it was still standing in its integrity, backed by all the resources of the mountains. Still less could one hope to smash with overt force the wide belt of fortresses and fortified auls that were enclosing Dagestan from our side while their inhabitants were ready for a vigorous defense. The losses would have been so enormous in such a venture, and success so doubtful, that it could not even be suggested.

The Chechens are undoubtedly the bravest people in the eastern mountains. The campaigns into their land have always cost us dearly. However, this tribe never quite internalized Muridism. Of all the eastern highlanders, the Chechens were the most independent in personal and social life, and they had forced Shamil, who ruled despotically in Dagestan, to make a thousand concessions to them in the way of government, in people's duties, and in the ritual strictness of their faith. Gazavat (war against the infidels) was only a pretext for them to defend their tribal independence and conduct raids. Many thousands of Chechens who had been deposed in 1840 have since resettled with us and enjoyed, under the exemplary administration created for them, a prosperity that tempted their fellow tribesmen. Shamil never trusted the Chechens, and did not consider them firmly committed to him. The disintegration of the mountain union founded by Muridism would most likely begin in Chechnya. Militarily, an offensive in this country was also more convenient. In Dagestan we encountered resistance at certain points which could not be avoided, while their capture always cost great sacrifices. In Chechnya, both lowland and highland, there was almost no place where the enemy could hold out against our onslaught; there it was always one skirmishing action on the move, if only our lines were strong enough to hold the enemy's attack. Having cleared the terrain in certain directions, it was possible to march through Chechnya without firing a shot; and with sufficient force, and a methodical mode of action, it is much easier to cut a clearing in a forest occupied by the enemy than to besiege a fortress where the defenders have settled in to the death, all the more so because the cleared terrain belongs to us forever, while an aul taken is only ours as long as it is occupied. We could reasonably expect that within a certain period of time we would cut through the forests that made up the Chechen stronghold and, having uncovered their dwellings, would force this bellicose but not fanatical people to submit, opening access through their land to the very depths of the mountains and thus coming to the rear of the strongholds on the Dagestan border.

Until then, expeditions were made periodically at certain times of the year, depending on the terrain; then the troops were disbanded to their quarters. This interval gave the mountaineers rest, which was absolutely necessary for them, since their strength consisted of the national militia, which had to be fed by their own labor. Prince Baryatinsky decided to wage war nonstop, allowing the mountaineers neither time nor rest until they were completely subdued. At the same time, he changed the very nature of the occupation of the conquered countries. Instead of towns erected at each new headquarters, the construction of which absorbed all the activity of the nominated troops for a long time, Prince Baryatinsky's plan was to build only a rampart at newly occupied points, placing troops in barracks and cabins, thus preserving their strength for war. These makeshift points could be abandoned once they had fulfilled their temporary purpose, and the troops could advance without interruption. We would firmly establish ourselves only at those points that would remain strategically important after the conquest of the mountains.

The distribution of troops by divisions was considered in view of the magnitude of the proposed actions. On the right flank and the three military divisions of the eastern Caucasus, in addition to the line battalions and Cossack troops, there was an infantry division, part of the Twenty-First Battalion, equal in strength to the two divisions now in operation. Of the Thirteenth and Eighteenth Divisions assigned, the first was divided by a brigade between the right flank, which was too extensive for a single division, and the left flank, from whence the main offensive was to be launched. The Eighteenth Division remained in the Caucasus as a reserve and available force for road works, the necessity of which was indicated by the previous war. (In 1859 the Thirteenth Infantry Division returned to its corps and was replaced by the Caucasian Reserve Division). Due to a lack of troops, the Kutaisi General Government would be occupied with only one brigade of line battalions, despite the extreme importance of this region, covering the entire Caucasus from the Black Sea, and the urgent need to develop it strategically.

The military actions were calculated with the above considerations in mind. On the Lezgin line our detachments were to annually ravage the enemy societies and bring them to exhaustion by the time of the decisive moment. In the Caspian region it was decided to first occupy Salatavia, which separated Dagestan from the eastern end of the left flank, in order to open the way to the mountains from the northern side and firmly bind the two armies by the time they would have to act together. On the left flank it was decided to first finish the conquest of the Chechen plain and stand firmly at the foot of the mountains; then to transfer the war to the mountains themselves, which had never yet seen Russian banners; to direct the first blow to the Argun gorge and, by occupying it up to the snowy ridge, to separate Lesser Chechnya from the greater and cut off the whole western corner of the country under the control of Muridism; and finally to move to Ichkeria, where Shamil's residence, Vedeno, was located, and thereby complete the conquest of the Chechens. When these conquests were accomplished and we would have a firm foot in the depths of the mountains, leaving only Dagestan to Shamil, we should move the whole mass of troops at once and finish the matter of Muridism with a single blow.

Such was the military plan of Prince Baryatinsky, which in three years solved the fifty-year struggle; it was a resolution for which the troops fighting against the mountaineers, and Russia at large, had long given up hope.

The occupation of the plain and the foothills (Greater Chechnya, Aukh, and Salatavia) was in fact only a preparatory action; it did not yet give us a clear advantage, but it created a new position from which we could launch a decisive offensive. The period of these preparatory actions covered the fall of 1856 and the whole of 1857.

During the first winter, from November to April, the troops of the left flank, led by General Yevdokimov, completed the network of clearing in Greater Chechnya (begun under Prince Vorontsov) in four campaigns and opened up this country in all directions, overcoming at every step the strong resistance of the Chechens supported by huge levies from Dagestan. The dense forests were felled in one winter. At the same time, a special detachment operating on the Kumyk plain under the command of General Baron Nikolai cleared the entrance to Aukh. The native population, scattered throughout the forests in small farms, remained in their homes, but Greater Chechnya was already like a fortress with its gates breached—its garrison would have to lay down its arms at the first request.

In the summer of 1857, the troops of the left flank did not advance. The operations were to open on the side of Dagestan and the Lezgin line, where the high terrain, covered with snow half of the year, is passable only in the summer months. During this time it was necessary to organize, in accordance with the new insights, the material situation of the left flank, where the position of fortifications and deployment of troops had gotten mixed up due to the successive replacement of administrative systems. The regiments of the left flank got to rest for the final time before embarking on a march which would not end until the last shot rang out in the eastern mountains.

The Dagestan and Lezgin detachments entered the mountains almost simultaneously. Adjutant General Prince Orbeliani was to establish a permanent headquarters for one of his regiments in Salatavia in order to connect the Caspian region with the left flank by direct communication and to give the Dagestan detachment a stronghold to advance into the mountains from the northern side. To fulfill this plan, it was necessary to overcome the stubborn resistance of the mountaineers. Salatavia was already flooded with enemy hordes under the personal leadership of Shamil. Prince Orbeliani quickly overcame the first obstacle—the Terengul ravine, so many times fruitlessly irrigated with Russian blood—and took a position on the other side near old Burtunai, recognized as convenient for the establishment of headquarters. The mountaineers, driven from the first position almost without a fight, scattered around the detachment and cut off our communications by arranging debris on the road from Burtunai to the Evgenievskoe fortification, from which the troops were supplied with food. A column detached from the camp drove them from this position and reopened communications, killing several hundred Murids on the spot. At this point Shamil occupied an impenetrable forested area four kilometers from the headquarters being erected, and began to build a fortress on his side which was to block ours permanently. Prince Orbeliani did not disturb him in this refuge until the autumn, caring only for the swift completion of the work undertaken by his own men. When the new headquarters was sufficiently established to receive troops for the winter, our detachment seized the enemy's fortifications in a surprise night movement and scattered them. A Dagestan infantry regiment was firmly established in Salatavia, but the Salatavians, who had scattered into the forests, were not yet subdued.

In the same summer, General Vrevsky crossed the mountain ridge from the Kakheti side and, in a few weeks, devastated most of the powerful Didoi community, burning auls and trampling the crops. This was the only possible course of action on the Lezgin line; it was not intended to conquer, but only to weaken the mountaineers and secure our borders. Exorbitant labor associated with the march to the highest, impassable part of the Caucasus and the impossibility of carrying sufficient food always reduced the term of the campaign on the Lezgin line and made it no more than a big raid. Distracted by Salatava affairs, Shamil left the defense of this part of the region to local forces, resulting in weak resistance from the enemy. A few Didoi held on in their towers and perished. Toward the end of the campaign, when our troops began their return journey, Shamil's son Ghazi Muhammad came to the rescue of the devastated region with a strong horde and tried to bypass our detachment. However, repulsed from the very first step, he was forced to watch motionlessly from the heights as our troops departed, leaving only ruins behind them. The Didoi population, driven to extremes, had to spend a brutal winter without shelter and food, living on handouts from neighboring societies. But hope for the future was not yet sufficiently shaken in the souls of the mountaineers; no one came to us from this distressed mass.

Muridism had so firmly united the social structure of the highlanders that for a whole year, from the fall of 1856 to the fall of 1857, in the course of inflicting on them a whole series of defeats and occupying locality after locality, we had not yet subdued a single person. But the resolve of the societies over which our blows fell most severely was already wavering, especially in Chechnya, which was less fanatical than the other tribes. With the opening of the winter operations, the turning point of the war began.

General Yevdokimov was to make the first step into the mountains during the winter by occupying the Argun gorge; but this campaign could be made only on the condition that there was no enemy in the rear of his advancing troops. The invasion of the mountains had to be preceded by a perfect conquest of the plain. In October 1857, General Yevdokimov suddenly ascended the Goyta river into the forest foothills, where the population of Lesser Chechnya lived, knocked off the plain by the expeditions of General Freytag. After a brief but bloody affair, the mountaineers were dispersed through the forests and their dwellings exterminated throughout the territory between the Goyta and Argun rivers. Having cleared the enemy from the right side of the proposed line of operations, General Yevdokimov crossed into Greater Chechnya and marched toward Michik, giving the appearance that all our forces were concentrating against the

Michik society. Shamil's hordes flocked to the defense of this naibstvo. Having convinced them that we were marching on Michik, General Yevdokimov quickly crossed the Kachkalykovsky ridge, joined the Kumyk detachment, and invaded Aukh, where access had been open since the previous year. This country was occupied in its entirety before the mountain horde standing on the Michik learned of the purpose of our maneuvers. The mountaineers now had to dislodge us from our firmly held positions rather than defend their land, a feat beyond their power. The Chechen detachment quietly cut a clearing through the Aukh forests and laid the Kishen-Aukh fortification deep inside them. Having completed this enterprise, General Yevdokimov moved again into Greater Chechnya, constantly separating the Chechen population living north of the great foothill clearing from Shamil's hordes, which he had pushed into the forested mountains to the south. Once in this position, he demanded obedience from the inhabitants of Greater Chechnya. Their country, which had been opened up by clearings since the previous year, was accessible from all directions; a Russian army stood between them and the Murids. Exhausted by seventeen years of war, and always cold to the cause of the corrective tariqat, the population of Greater Chechnya submitted and was resettled on the left bank of the Argun.

With both sides of the Argun gorge cleared of the enemy and our rear secure, we could finally enter the mountains. In January 1858, General Yevdokimov approached the Argun gate, where the enemy had concentrated his forces in strong barricades. The battle might have been extremely bloody, but skillful detouring delivered us the mountain fortifications without loss. Having taken possession of the valley formed behind the Argun gate by the confluence of the two rivers, the Chantiy-Argun and the Sharo-Argun, General Yevdokimov laid here a fortification called the Argun fortification, which was to serve as the initial stage in the conquest of the mountains. The new fortification grew from the snow with unusual speed. With the first thaw, the main Chechen detachment could move on.

To the left of the Argun fortification, from the bank of the Sharo-Argun, rises the high ridge of Dargin-Duk, covered with dense forest on the slopes but bare at the top; further on, this ridge connects with the Andian mountains and leads several high, conveniently passable mountain glades to the rear of Ichkeria and Vedeno, Shamil's capital. Having completed the fortifications, General Yevdokimov abruptly climbed to the top of Dargin-Duk, preventing enemy resistance in an area that would have been impassable with sufficient defenses; having taken commanding positions, the Chechen detachment cut through the clearing without a shot, allowing us free access to this natural mountain road. The Dargin-Duk Road accomplished two goals simultaneously. If it was found more advantageous to bypass Ichkeria, it led us to the rear of this country by a convenient road; if it was found better to act in another direction, the danger to which the mountaineers were exposed by the newly opened road still drew their attention and forces to Dargin-Duk, which greatly eased our ventures.

As soon as the Chechen detachment returned from the ridge to the Argun valley, the mountaineers immediately occupied Dargin-Duk in a strong cluster and began to block the road with ditches and fortifications. Leaving them to sit quietly on this perch, General Yevdokimov rushed across the Argun valley to the rear of the small Chechen auls, which had been dealt a heavy blow last autumn. This tribe realized its fate and submitted. It could not go farther into the mountains, which were populated by other societies who valued their land. The inhabitants of Greater Chechnya, who had been hiding in the forest foothills for more than 10 years, and who had made incessant raids into our borders from there, were evicted to their former locations, between the mountains and the Sunzha.

The winter actions of 1857–1858 ended with the conquest of Lesser Chechnya; the northern plains and foothills were conquered and the entrance to the mountains was opened. With summer began new campaigns deep into the mountains which would crush Muridism within fifteen months. However, despite the bold direction of our troops into the heart of those slums, which were unknown until then and considered inaccessible, these expeditions had to be carried out methodically for another year, developing the terrain at every step and considering as ours only the land on which the enemy could no longer resist. The mountainous alliance, which remained active only at the edges, was still too strong to be confronted directly.

In June, troops were to move into the mountains from all three directions: the Chechen detachment up the Chantiy-Argun gorge; the Dagestani from Burtunai to Michik, threatening to invade Andia; and the Lezgin through Kanucha into the inner mountains of Lezgistan, lying east of the Didoi society. The main operation was entrusted to the Chechen detachment, which was to occupy the course of the Argun to the snowy ridge. The Dagestani detachment carried out only sabotage. The Lezgin detachment, now combined, was to both keep the enemy occupied and continue the enterprise they had begun—the ravaging of the unruly societies of southern Lezgistan.

In the meantime the old imam, constrained as he had never been before and finally seeing our true aspirations, endeavored to renew the means which had been successful for him so many times before—to kindle a popular uprising in our rear. Muridic propaganda set to work among the peaceful population, as in the 1840s, but on the side of the mountaineers there was no longer the same infatuation kindled by good fortune, and the most ardent adherents of the corrective tariqat did not dare to start an uprising. The Nazran society, which had long been peaceful, though restless and predatory, living near Vladikavkaz, was ordered to settle in large auls following the example of the Chechens because of the proven impossibility of managing a mountain population scattered in small hamlets. Their spirits ignited by Shamil's agents, the Nazranians became indignant. A joyous clamor answered their revolt in all the mountains; until then, a spark was enough to start a fire. Shamil, prepared in advance, rushed toward Nazran through Lesser Chechnya, hoping that this tribe, which had just been conquered, would be carried away by the example of its neighbors. But our side also took measures in advance. Columns, closely networked around the foothills, instantly drew to the point where Shamil came to the plain and pushed him back. At the same time, Nazran was subdued by arms. The movements necessitated by this incident did not slow down a single day of the projected expedition.

The Chechen detachment had to conquer the most impregnable terrain, perhaps in the entire Caucasus. Up the Argun lay the rich Shatoy valley, the occupation of which was half the solution; but it was behind a ridge with only one path leading to it, along the right side of a blind gorge dug by the Argun into the highest mountains. One landslide could stop a whole army here. Both the mountains and the gorge were clothed with dense forest, without a trail or a road. While the detachment was being assembled, our troops made several demonstrations at the foot of Dargin-Duk, finally leaving the mountaineers resigned to the fact that the Russians would take this path. The main enemy horde was positioned above the Dargin-Duk clearing, from where it could not reach the Shatoy road in time, but the Chantiy-Argun gorge was also occupied by a party of several hundred men, quite sufficient to keep us out. General Yevdokimov led a clearing into the gorge; the mountain naibs, well aware of the impassability of this terrain, took our maneuver for a demonstration and became even more vigilant in guarding the Dargin-Duk. Waiting until nightfall, General Yevdokimov transferred the detachment to the left bank of the Argun by way of a bridge secretly arranged in a deep trough of the river, and with dawn rushed for the Shatoy valley, without a road, straight through the forest ridge of Miken-Duk. This strategy by the Chechen detachment relied entirely on secrecy and calculation of the time it would take for the mountaineers to cross the Argun and climb a high ridge, because meeting a significant number of the enemy in the Miken-Duk forest would have meant a defeat for us. The calculation was correct. Only a few locals put up a struggle, and the head of the detachment had already reached the Varandy clearing when the first panting crowd of mountaineers appeared. The Murids had to return to the gorge without a fight.

The main obstacle had been overcome, but behind the detachment lay the Miken-Duk forest, through which a road had to be built. For almost an entire month, the Chechen detachment developed a road back through the gorge they had bypassed and forward to the Shatoy valley. In the meantime, our columns entered the mountains from the other directions as well. The Dagestan detachment, led by Adjutant General Baron Wrangel, who had taken the place of Prince Orbeliani, moved toward Michik, destroying the blockades that were obstructing access to Andia. General Vrevsky crossed the snowy ridge with the Lezgin detachment and penetrated the lands of the Capuchin society, while another small detachment, operating from the same side, moved toward General Yevdokimov on the upper reaches of the Argun. Attacked at once from several sides, the experienced leader of Muridism immediately realized where the main blow was coming from, and, leaving his followers in charge at other points, turned with his sons and principal corps against General Yevdokimov. The mountaineers had taken an extremely strong position near the aul of Bol'shiye Varandy, covering the only access to the Shatoy valley. However, Shamil, schooled by experience, no longer trusted strong positions; knowing what further Russian movement inland would lead to, he decided to stop it by invading our borders. Leaving half of his numerous troops at the position in front of Shatoy, the imam rushed with the other half to Vladikavkaz, where he hoped to find allies in the Nazrans; with luck, Shamil could take the upper hand over our weak troops there, which would lead to an uprising of the tribes of the entire central Caucasus who still believed in Muridism. But luck had long since betrayed the old military leader; his brave intention proved to be his undoing. General Yevdokimov, leading a march deep into the mountains, arranged the columns on the plain in such a way that they mutually supported one another and could concentrate on any threatened point. On the same day Shamil, who had come down to the flat near Vladikavkaz, was defeated by General Mishchenko; General Yevdokimov, taking advantage of the imam's absence, dispersed the hordes occupying the Varandy position and took possession of Shatoy. Shamil was cut off and had to ascend the Argun almost to the snowy ridge, only to escape home.

It was then that the entire highland Chechen population, community by community, revolted against Muridism. Preventing the movement of our columns, the inhabitants of the Argun region began to expel and slaughter their naibs, clerics, and all Dagestanis, whatever rank they held. One after another, the Chechen tribes sent deputies to General Yevdokimov with a declaration of submission. This movement spread far and wide, even to such tribes that we could not hope to support because of their remoteness and whom, therefore, we had to advise that they wait for a more favorable time. The Chechens were avenging Muridism for the eighteen years of oppression that had crushed their willful personality, and with their characteristic ardor they sincerely extended their hand to us. Of the entire Chechen population, Shamil now had only Ichkeria, which he ruled personally, and the half-Chechen, half-Avar society of the Cheberloy. However, he could no longer be in doubt that these tribes too, at the first appearance of the Russians, would follow the general movement.

At the end of October 1858, a vast area of mountains from the Georgian Military Road to the Sharo-Argun recognized Russian power. A convenient road was developed for free movement of troops along the Chantiy-Argun valley, protected by three fortifications. A headquarters for the Navaginsky infantry regiment was established in Shatoy. All that remained was to open up the newly acquired region by longitudinal routes and to put in order the small brigand societies that inhabited its western end.

While the actions on the Argun were taking place, General Baron Vrevsky crossed the snowy ridge and, passing through the Capuchin society, invaded the inner lands of Ankratl, where Russian arms had never before penetrated. The main forces of Shamil were far away, but the numerous local population, remembering the previous year's devastation of the Didoi society and fearing a similar fate for themselves, flocked under the banners of their naibs, fiercely contesting every step of the advancing detachment. The obstacles to our movement in this region, imposed by nature and the persistence of the inhabitants, were extraordinary. Cloudy ridges, bottomless precipices, forests, and stone auls formed an almost impenetrable labyrinth, where every inch of land was a Lezgin fortress. Throughout the entire campaign, our troops had to fight their way forward with open force, crossing wobbling bridges hanging over the abyss to storm cliffs fenced with rubble. In spite of the stubborn resistance of the Lezgins who defended this terrain, our detachment devastated seven communities of Ankratl within five weeks, destroyed more than forty stone auls, and took three fortifications with artillery. Yet the success of this expedition cost us dearly. At the seizure of the aul of Kituri, General Vrevsky and several excellent officers were mortally wounded. Taking charge of the detachment, Colonel Korganov continued the offensive, ravaged the last Didoi auls left on the eastern borders of this community from last year's extermination, and only then descended from the mountains. The double devastation and loss of faith in Shamil, who had suffered defeats all summer, had their effect on the inhabitants of impregnable Lezgistan. Seeing the impossibility of repelling our blows and not daring to submit their land to us, which with the onset of autumn we could not protect, four thousand Antsukhs and Capuchins moved from the mountains to our territory.

The movement of Adjutant General Baron Wrangel to Michik was, as has already been said, only a demonstration intended to divert Shamil's forces and attention from Shatoy. The time had not yet come for a decisive offensive from Dagestan. In 1858, the Dagestan troops had to perform a lot of unseen, though very important, work; it was necessary to achieve the goal for which Salatavia was occupied: the development of routes from Burtunai to Aukh and the Kumyk plain. By conquering Salatavia, the troops of the Caspian region and the left flank were connected into one active force, concentrated against the northern side of the mountains, but in order for them to truly unite it was necessary to establish several roads from Burtunai to the extremities of the country, to gather the scattered and hitherto still hostile Salatavian population, and to subdue the Aukhovians, who stubbornly held on to their forest farms. The Salatava detachment was busy in the execution of these enterprises throughout the summer of 1858 and all of the following winter. Besides the actions in Salatavia, the Dagestan troops had to guard the long frontier line from the Sulak to the snowy ridge. With the base in Burtunai, the main forces of the Caspian region were concentrated in the northwestern corner of this country, which made it necessary to weaken the defensive means of Dagestan itself; all the while, no matter how constrained the enemy was, he had greater forces and the necessity of desperate measures could direct him toward the subdued Dagestan, as it had driven him to the side of Vladikavkaz earlier that year. In the Caspian region it was necessary to act very cautiously.

The main actions that winter, as well as during the previous summer, were to be performed by General Yevdokimov. With the occupation of the Argun region, the troops of the left flank were spread over too vast an area, yet they were responsible for the execution of the most important enterprises. The commander-in-chief reinforced the left flank with eight battalions from the grenadiers and the Eighteenth Infantry Division. With these reinforcements, General Yevdokimov could divide his forces. Leaving a detachment on the Argun, sufficient to cover the recent conquest and the new Chechen settlements, he concentrated other troops in Galashki, at the western tip of the Chechen-occupied country near the limits of the Ossetian military district. The Galashki detachment proceeded to develop this remote country, which had hitherto been one hopeless wilderness harboring brigand villages and fugitives. The troops cleared the glades; but it was impossible for them to overtake the small population of Abreks who hid themselves in the wildest places. To resolve this problem, General Yevdokimov sent two thousand horsemen from the newly conquered population of Lesser Chechnya into the mountains under the leadership of their naib. The Chechens scattered into the forests, exterminated the persistent brigands, and forced the others to move to the flatlands. By the end of the year this part of the region was uncovered and pacified.

While General Yevdokimov was within the Ossetian military district, Shamil, his activity increasing with the calamities that befell him, planned a new campaign, hoping to expel us from the newly-conquered Argun region. Meanwhile, we had laid the Yevdokimov fortification above the Shatoy fortification, which now marked the highest point of our line on the Argun; beyond it began the spurs of the snowy ridge, which blocked any passage for an army at this time of year. Between the Shatoy and Yevdokimov fortifications, the Argun flowed through a rocky fissure of immeasurable depth, wherein the only path connecting the two fortifications curved along the rocky ledges. Shamil positioned a strong force in the foothills of Greater Chechnya with the aim of attracting our troops to that side, and with another party rushed suddenly to the gorge between the Shatoy and Yevdokimov fortifications; he hoped to capture the gorge, cut through our forces stretched along the Argun, and open access to the trans-Argun region, where rapid movements were impossible for regular troops at this time of year. He ordered the forces left in Chechnya to rush to the same point at the first report of his success. Shamil's plan was conceived with a true military outlook and could have put us in a difficult position. But the Murids were operating in the midst of a Chechen population that had already broken its moral alliance with them. Their movements could not remain a secret from us. Shamil met our battalions at points he had hoped to capture by surprise, and had to abandon his daring enterprise.

Ichkeria was the only place left before the entire Chechen nation could be considered subdued. Shamil foresaw where our forces would go and spent a whole year fortifying his capital, Vedeno. Not counting on the natives, he summoned assemblies from all Dagestan for the defense of Ichkeria. Before Christmas, General Yevdokimov moved three detachments to Ichkeria. The first detachment, under his personal leadership, entered the Bass river gorge from Shali; the second, under Colonel Bazhanov, headed for the same river through the mountains from the Argun fortification; Prince Mirsky led the third detachment from the Kumyk plain through Greater Chechnya. By New Year's Day the detachments converged on the Bass river. Our troops, as they moved forward, cut down the forest and paved the road. The Dagestanis fought stubbornly, never giving up that foreign land without a fight, but the Ichkerian Chechens resisted only under the eyes of their allies and surrendered as soon as the Dagestanis were forced to retreat from their dwellings. In three weeks, up to a thousand families of this tribe were evicted to the plains. Moving up the Bass gorge, the Chechen detachment approached a strong position in the Tauzen tract, fortified in advance by the enemy. General Yevdokimov sent a column to bypass the blockades on the snow-covered mountains; when its arrival on the ridge above Tauzen spread hesitation among the mountaineers, General Kemfert, who approached the position from the front, struck them down in one swift blow. After this affair, the development of the terrain again required considerable effort. Early in February, the Bass gorge was cleared as far as the aul of Alistanzhi, the point from which the road to Vedeno emerges from the gorge into the mountains. This part of the country presented to the highlanders every advantage for a strong defense. General Yevdokimov chose to make his way to Vedeno at once, placing his troops in a fortified camp in front of the enemy's fortress, and then to develop the road to the rear. A special column was sent along the ridges to take a detour flanking the line along which the main forces were to advance. This maneuver, executed quickly, opened the way to Vedeno. Our troops occupied a mountain two kilometers from Shamil's fortified residence. Here the Chechen detachment was to halt until a convenient connection to our borders opened in the rear of the position. Having knocked down the mountaineers from the surrounding heights, General Yevdokimov fenced his camps with traps and began to build a road back along the route he had taken. The inclement weather made the work extremely difficult. As the troops in front of Vedeno built a fortress, gradually rising in the enemy's sight, the road to Bass was washed away several times by rain, not finished and dry until mid-March. Only then, with the arrival of artillery (the Chechen detachment had nothing but mountain guns until then), could the siege begin.

Vedeno is situated in a valley, at the junction of two deep ravines that enclose it from the northern side, whence our troops arrived. From the east it is flanked by a chain of hillocks, gradually descending from the ridge; on this chain a number of closed redoubts were built by the mountaineers. The mountain fortifications consisted of ditches, palisades, dugouts, round bastions, and tall, thick ramparts made of logs piled with earth as cover for riflemen. Vedeno was occupied by a garrison of seven thousand men under the command of fourteen naibs subordinate to Shamil's son Ghazi Muhammad. On March 17th and 18th, the first trenches were laid, one on the western side of the fortress, the other against the separate Andian fortification, which blocked the line of redoubts from our side. A special column was placed to interrupt the communication of the enemy garrison with Ichkeria; his only route for retreat was now Andia, which was not blocked by Russian troops so as not to push the resistance of the mountaineers to the extreme. The main forces of the enemy's fortifications were in the line of redoubts surrounding Vedeno from the east; they commanded the fortress itself, so it would be necessary to storm it and remain within in it after the assault under their fire. In order to disrupt this line, all we had to do was to position ourselves at the same height, occupying one of the redoubts. In the last days of March, our attack was brought from the western side to the ravine, whence our artillery shelled the foot of the redoubts facing the fortress and tore the enemy garrison into two halves without communication; from the east it moved sixty paces to the Andian redoubt. On April 1st, an assault column under the command of General Kemfert was appointed. At sunset, after a heavy cannonade which covered the Andian redoubt with shells, it was stormed and taken instantly. It happened as General Yevdokimov had intended. The garrison of the neighboring redoubt, seeing the incomparably superior forces of the assailants near themselves and on the same height, found resistance impossible and retreated to the redoubt lying further away. This retreat was communicated to the whole line, and in two hours the redoubts were abandoned by the enemy. From that moment, Shamil's fortress was open to fire from above. The movement of Colonel Chertkov's column along the Hulkhulau gorge to the only line of retreat remaining for the mountaineers ended the matter. The enemy set fire to the fortress and retreated up the mountain. After the bloody battles of the previous era, which had cost so many thousands of men, the assault that decided the fate of Vedeno cost only twenty-six men removed from the line.

While the siege of Vedeno was in progress, Adjutant

General Baron Wrangel entered Ichkeria from the east, in order to clear glades in the very places through which our troops had retreated from Dargo in 1845. New clearings were made on this side. By the beginning of summer, Ichkeria had been uncovered and the population of that country, the Aukh and the natives of Greater Chechnya who had fled from our power in the forest foothills, had been subdued by the ceaseless actions of the Chechen and Salatava detachments which scattered their columns in all directions. Greater Chechnya was repopulated by its former inhabitants, gathered in large auls. Perfect safety, even for a solitary traveler, was established throughout the newly conquered region.

After the conquest of Vedeno, the considerable Gaberloe society, Shamil's last Chechen land, rebelled against his authority without waiting for Russian columns, expelling the Murids and sending a delegation to General Yevdokimov.

The entire Chechen nation, down to the last village, was subdued. Dagestan alone was left to Shamil. But as long as Dagestan stood under the banner of Muridism, our dominance in the Caucasus remained as precarious within Chechnya as outside it. In Dagestan lay the spiritual center of the Muslim revolt.

This vast, unapproachable region, unknown at its depths, inhabited by bellicose and viciously fanatical tribes slavishly submissive to spiritual authority, could defend its independence without Chechen assistance, as had been proved in previous years. During the Akhulgo campaign, even before the Chechen uprising, when we controlled the loyal Avaria and Koysubu in the middle of the mountains, when not all Dagestani tribes stood for Muridism, the main forces of the Caucasian Corps were sent against Shamil from both sides. At that time the Russian troops had laid down five thousand men before one village, the destruction of which was the only result of the campaign. Now the whole of Dagestan, organized and furnished with fortresses, obeyed Shamil; the forces of Muridism were much more significant than in 1839. The difference consisted only in our relative position and that of the enemy; but in this difference lay the subsequent fate of the war. The conquests of the two preceding years had radically changed the strategic conditions of the offensive on Dagestan and deeply shaken the confidence of the mountain population in the invincibility of their refuges. Until now we could only penetrate Dagestan from two sides: the south and the east. The southern side was protected by a snowy ridge, behind which it was impossible to establish a foothold; the eastern side by a wide defensive strip, where the long war had turned every village into a fortress. Here and there the advancing troops had to push the mountaineers from the circumference to the center, into the unexplored depths of the region, too vast to be traversed at once; with every step inland the forces of the mountaineers increased, and for us the difficulties of food and communication increased. These conditions had hitherto made only methodical warfare possible in the mountains. With the conquest of the Argun region and Ichkeria, we exposed a third side of Dagestan where nothing was prepared for a vigorous defense—neither the people nor their dwellings; we placed made our military base near the very depths of the unknown mountains on which the border tribes relied. The experience of the Lezgin Campaigns had already shown how weak the resistance of the highlanders inside Dagestan was—a detachment that stormed three auls a day there would not be enough to besiege one village on the eastern border. At any rate, on the northern side, opened by the recent conquests, the natural defenses of Dagestan were no stronger than the Lezgin line with the cover of the snowy ridge removed. Moreover, entering Dagestan from this side, we seized the very heart of the region from the first step and pressed the mountaineers from their core, pushing them over our frontier lines and entering the rear of their strongholds. This new strategic position was the consequence and goal of all the previous campaigns. While the conquest of Chechnya was taking place, the troops of the Caspian region were consolidating themselves in Salatavia; by the summer of 1859, the former principle of attacking Dagestan from the sea was already abandoned. Both the left flank and the Dagestan detachment were concentrated in firmly occupied points on one line, against the northern, newly opened side of the mountains. Only the Lezgin line detachment, operating from the Georgian side, was by necessity a separate mass.

The self-confidence of the mountain population, which for so long had been the strength of Muridism, was deeply shaken by recent events. In 1858 and the first months of 1859 all defeats fell on the Tavlins, because the Chechen population, which had already had its turn, avoided fighting as much as possible and submitted at the first sign of success on our side. While fighting in a foreign land, the Tavlins had learned how firmly the Russian troops held the positions entrusted to their defense; they could not expect anything else for themselves at home. The people's enthusiasm and determination to defend themselves to the death were sustained by the certainty that we could be repulsed; with the fall of this certainty, the energy of the masses weakened. Meanwhile, Shamil remained with his firmly established power, supported by all the sworn members of Muridism, i.e., the entire thinking part of the population emerging from the popular crowd. In fact, Shamil had even more at his disposal: he could deploy many thousands of brave soldiers against us, had faithful and experienced assistants, impregnable fortresses, and considerable material resources. Yet, as the hope of fighting off the Russians waned, every highlander naturally began to think of himself, of his family, and of his property. There was no doubt that the crowds gathered under the eyes of Shamil or his chief naibs would fight resolutely; but with the weakening of the people's faith in success these crowds became troops, in a certain sense of the word, troops who would no longer fight for every stone; they could be attacked on purely strategic considerations, as in any other war, and the matter could be settled by a rapid invasion.

This is clear now. But that June, Dagestan still seemed an impassable backwater; so fresh was the memory of the bloody and futile attempts that had been repeated against this land for twenty consecutive years, that it seemed impossible to end the matter at once. No one doubted that it was now possible to break Dagestan, but to break it in several steps, methodically, as it had happened in Chechnya, calculating the actions for a certain number of years. Everyone was then convinced of this, positively everyone except one man; fortunately, that man was the commander-in-chief. The conquest of Dagestan was accomplished in five weeks, forever ridding the Caucasus of the Muridism that had been gnawing at its insides like a cancer.

The general offensive was supposed to begin on all sides simultaneously, in the first days of July. The main Chechen detachment of 14,000 men under the personal command of Count Yevdokimov was concentrated near Vedeno; Colonel Kaufman's smaller detachment of the left flank was preparing to march from Shatoy. The main detachment in the Caspian region, the Salatava detachment—consisting of about 9,000, to be further reinforced afterward—assembled at Burtunai. All these troops, amounting to about 25,000 bayonets and horses, were appointed to make an attack from the northern side of the mountains. The eastern side of Dagestan, facing the Caspian Sea, was guarded by a detachment of five battalions stationed at Turchidag under the command of General Prince Tarkhanov, ready now to take the offensive. About 2,000 men were also ready to move from Temir-Khan-Shura, if necessary, into the gap between the Salatava and Turchidag detachments. These three detachments were at the disposal of Adjutant General Baron Wrangel, who was attached to the Salatava detachment. A detachment of 7,000 men was concentrated on the Lezgin line under the command of General Prince Melikov, flanked by two small detachments from the side of the fortress of Novi Zakatal and Tusheti led by Princes Shalikov and

Cholokashvili. The whole mass of troops, assembled with the greatest efforts to advance into the mountains on three sides, did not exceed 40,000 armed men out of the 240,000 that made up the Caucasian army in those months (out of 160,000, if we do not count the troops of the right flank and of the governor-general of Kutaisi). This is a striking example of the localization—one might say absorption—of troops for the needs of a minor defense and occupation of the region, which were a consequence of the Caucasian War.

The actions of the three detachments—the Chechen, Dagestan, and Lezgin detachments, flanked by secondary columns dependent on them—were subordinated to one general plan, but each commander was independent in his military theater and guided by local considerations to achieve his objectives. The greatest strength of the enemy's defense consisted of the Andi Koysu line, which covered the unruly mountains from the north, firmly fortified and occupied by numerous clusters of mountaineers. This line stopped the advance of the Chechen and Dagestani detachments almost from their first step into the mountains. The Lezgin detachment, operating from the southern side, was somewhat in the rear of this line. In accordance with Prince Baryatinsky's plan, the detachments were to converge against the middle course of the Andi Koysu river, destroying the defensive line of the mountaineers with their combined efforts. The main, though passive, role in the general offensive belonged to the Chechen detachment, which pressed against the most impregnable section of the enemy line; the commander-in-chief himself had come to these troops to be at the center of the action. The Chechen detachment, the largest of the three, took the shortest route to the middle reaches of the Andi Koysu; after some time, when the other columns delved deeper into the mountains, it was to become a connecting and supporting mass for all the advancing troops. The presence of the commander-in-chief and the very destination of the Chechen detachment—into the heart of the unruly land—caused the Murids to give all their attention to this part of our forces; anticipating a decisive blow from it, they coordinated their actions with its actions. Moving slowly, without revealing his intentions, the commander-in-chief confused Shamil and forced him to keep his forces together; this made it easier for the flank detachments to deliver a sudden blow to the mountaineers. It was enough for one of them to reach the right bank of the Andi Koysu to overthrow the whole defensive system of the enemy. It was anticipated that the Dagestan detachment would play the active role. It advanced alongside the Chechen detachment, with both sides enjoying equal success. The enemy had fewer forces stationed downstream than in the middle part of the Koysu. Across the river, opposite the Gumbet mountain, lay Koysubu and Avaria, societies that had stood firmly with us in 1843 and suffered a long persecution from Shamil. Having broken across the river in the lower part of its course, we were entering directly into this region, the only place in Dagestan where we could count on an amiable reception. With the uprising of Avaria in Dagestan, the same decomposition that delivered Chechnya to us was expected to begin. In any case, with or without Avaria's assistance, once the Dagestan detachment had broken across the river, it was only necessary for it to extend its right flank up the riverbank to take the fortifications piled up by the mountaineers against Tekhnutsal in the rear. Then the Chechen detachment could freely cross the Koysu and lend a hand to the Lezgin detachment, which until then had been separated as if by an abyss from the forces operating in the north. However, if the Dagestan detachment met insurmountable obstacles from its side, in this extreme case the Lezgin detachment could penetrate deep into the mountains and reach the rear of the enemy line, though with much greater risk and considerable expense of time. In any case, one or the other had to bypass Shamil and seize the crossing of the Koysu. Then all three detachments would connect in the heart of the mountains and the outcome of the struggle would become certain; all that remained was to pursue Shamil quickly, not allowing him to establish himself in any part of the region.

The plan was for the Chechen detachment to act methodically at the beginning of the campaign, developing the road from Vedeno to Andia; for the Lezgin detachment to continue the system to which it had already adhered for two years—to ravage the enemy's territory, moving little by little into the interior of the mountains; and for the Dagestan detachment alone to make a decisive offensive from the very first step. As Count Yevdokimov had been entrusted with the execution of the commander-in-chief's plans of methodical warfare, so now Baron Wrangel was entrusted with the task of inflicting swift and final blows on Muridism.

The northern side of Dagestan, on which the combined forces of the left flank and the Pre-Caspian region were advancing, is enclosed by an extremely high, though not snow-capped, ridge, which stretches in a continuous wall to the northeast, from Khevsureti to Salatavia, separating the Chechen population from the Tavlin. Beyond the ridge, at a distance of fifteen to twenty kilometers, the Andi Koysu flows in the deepest abyss. There are no gorges across the ridge; one has to climb to its summit and then descend again into the terrible depths. The river can be crossed only in a few places, where there are paths leading to the riverbed at an oblique angle along steep cliffs. The long strip between the ridge and the river is cut into several separate cells by the buttresses of the ridge, which reach to the very bank of the Koysu. Shamil arranged the defense of this country with a perceptive military eye. The troops of the left flank and the Pre-Caspian region were to advance separately, each supported by their own military and food base, one in the recently conquered Ichkeria, the other in Salatavia. Before the Chechen detachment lay Andia, before the Dagestani Gumbet, separated by a high buttress, through which only two routes connected the lands: the upper, through the so-called Andia Gate, and the lower, over the river. Shamil fortified the right bank of the Koysu and the buttress perpendicular to the river. Opposite the Tekhnutsal valley, near the village of Konkhidat where the Chechen detachment was to descend, the mountaineers built a whole system of fortifications, stone walls with loopholes, and batteries, eight kilometers long. It was almost impossible to take these fortifications by force with the raging river serving as a natural moat. Further, at a considerable distance, the Koysu is impassable due to the terrain itself. Opposite Gumbet, along the path of the Dagestan detachment's advance, Shamil fortified the Sogritlokh bridge with armored galleries, hidden in the rocks and inaccessible from any side, even for artillery fire. He left bridges across the Koysu only in places inaccessible to us, enclosing them with rubble. On the rest of the stream not only were the bridges removed, but even the rocks above the river were broken off. The upper route connecting Andia and Tekhnutsal with Gumbet was blocked by towers and debris in the Andia gate and on the neighboring paths. On the lower path, where the buttress rests on the river, Shamil fortified the Kilitli mountain and positioned himself on it with his main forces. The entire population of Andia, Tekhnutsal, and Gumbet were forced to move their families and livestock to the other side of the river and burn their auls. With these defenses, all strategic advantages belonged to the mountaineers. From the first step into the enemy's land, the Dagestan and Chechen detachments were separated by the buttress occupied by the mountaineers and faced an almost insurmountable obstacle—the Andi Koysu; meanwhile the enemy could refuse to fight whenever he wanted, locking himself in his fortifications; he could also direct the whole mass of his forces against the separated detachments or the columns they were sending out, without any fear for the rear and flanks. The military theater lying in front of our detachments was a chessboard in which all the borders between the squares were occupied by the enemy. We had only one advantage—the tactical superiority of our troops. If it was possible to find an opportunity somewhere to exploit this advantage and break through the enemy's defensive network at a single point, the matter was won, because the highlanders could not regain their lost advantage through open combat. The forthcoming actions were planned with this in mind.

By July 1st, the head of the general staff, the chiefs of the army's special arms, and the field staff had gathered in the fortress of Grozny. On July 4, the commander-in-chief arrived to the troops, directly from St. Petersburg, where he had gone for a short time. A few days later the offensive began.

On July 14th, the main Chechen detachment left Vedeno and encamped near Lake Yaniam. For two days in succession, the commander-in-chief conducted reconnaissance to the Andian side. On the 17th the detachment moved to Lake Retlo. On the 18th, extensive reconnaissance was conducted again. At this time Shamil was burning Andian and Tekhnutsal villages. On the 22nd the Chechen detachment advanced and encamped on the edge of the Andian ridge, above the Tekhnutsal valley. At every stop the troops developed a road for wheeled vehicles through the mountains. Shamil tensely followed the actions of the main detachment from his fortified position. Meanwhile, the fate of the first half of the campaign was already decided at another location.

Adjutant General Baron Wrangel took up a position near Michik, on the northern foot of Gumbet ridge, in the first days of July. Having received here the commander-in-chief's latest instructions, he moved forward on the same day as the Chechen detachment: July 14th. Behind the ridge, in the path of the detachment, the mountaineers occupied Arguani, a strong aul, the capture of which in 1839 had cost us eight hundred men; but the Dagestan detachment, having reached the last peaks of the ridge, headed along the spur overlooking the rear of the village. The mountaineers had to abandon this position without a fight. From the heights near Arguani the position of at least half of Shamil's hordes was revealed. They were crowded together at the Andi Gate and all along the buttress, apparently expecting that the Dagestan detachment would forcefully open communications with the Chechen one. No one was visible across the river; owning several bridges, the mountaineers could cross from one bank to the other without hindrance, so they had not bothered to occupy the opposite side beforehand. Not wasting a minute, Baron Wrangel took advantage of this blunder. In spite of the extreme fatigue of the troops after the strenuous trek through the mountains, Baron Wrangel immediately moved a column under the command of General Rakussa to the Sogritlokh bridge, knowing that his soldiers would always have strength when there was a crucial task before them. These troops found the bridge removed and the surrounding terrain such that the river could only be approached with proper operations, under deadly enemy fire; consequently, they could not cross the river immediately. But on the next morning a place was found, a kilometer downstream, to which the highlanders had not paid attention, and where it was possible, though with the greatest difficulty, to make a bridge. On both sides the banks were totally sheer, making it impossible to go down to the water. Arriving at the advanced position, General Wrangel decided to cross at this point. The troops occupied the heights of the left bank and immediately covered them with obstructions for riflemen and artillery before the enemy could occupy the opposite side with considerable force. From that moment we controlled the crossing; our fire covered the other bank to such an extent that, when the late hordes of mountaineers arrived at Sogritlokh with their guns, they could neither descend to the river, nor build blockades against us, nor strike at the head of the crossing column; their action was limited to shelling the camp and the crossing from the surrounding mountains. The only thing left to do was to control the raging river, but this was the most difficult part of the affair. All the material means for the crossing, brought on the soldiers' backs, consisted of ropes and a few planks. For two days the work proved futile. A few men crossed in a cradle conveyed over the abyss on a rope and encamped in a cave on the opposite bank, slaughtering the Murids who defended it. But it would be impossible to ferry the entire detachment by rope, and meanwhile the highland hordes were increasing by the hour until they covered all the surrounding mountains. It was only on the third day that a shaky rope plait fifteen fathoms long and a few kilometers wide was thrown across the Koysu, on which the men could cross one by one. At daybreak several companies converged on the other bank and boldly marched to the rear of the galleries enclosing the Sogritlokh bridge. Despite the extreme numerical superiority, the mountaineers avoided open combat and retreated to the mountains. A permanent bridge was immediately built at Sogritlokh, where the cliffs above the river nearly meet.

To open access to Avaria, the only thing left to do was to take the Akhkent mountain, which rises steeply above the river and was already surrounded by blockades. On July 21st, as soon as communication between the two banks was firmly established, Baron Wrangel advanced an assault column under the command of General Rakussa. The troops had to climb up a winding path to two enormously high escarpments and through a dense forest, then climb to the top of a steep stone ridge, from which a series of high mountain glades stretches all the way to Avaria. The troops moved before dawn, climbing the first ledge and knocking the enemy back from below, finally breaking through the forest; but here they saw strong blockades with loopholes and turbastions before them, which could not be approached except by slowly climbing the slope under heavy enemy fire; the success of the assault was doubtful, and the loss would inevitably be great. With the swiftness and self-confidence that distinguish the Caucasian soldier, the battalions turned to the right and climbed straight up the ridge they were passing under. Soldiers climbed up the abrupt cliff, pushing each other up, clinging to the crevices and plants sprouting in the rock, under a hail of stones thrown on their heads; in an hour the front battalions were already on the top; the mountaineers fled from the bypassed blockades. The same evening, the Dagestan detachment conquered the village of Tsatanykh, where our fortification once stood, taken by Shamil in 1843.

On July 22nd, the entire Dagestan detachment camped on the mountains near the village of Akhkent. When the troops were pitching tents, the Tsatanians came to the camp to ask for help against a party of Murids threatening them. The party turned out to be a delegation from all the Avar villages sent to Baron Wrangel. The Avars said: "We have been gnawing on Shamil's irons for sixteen years, waiting for you to give us a hand. Now the end of his kingdom has come."

While Baron Wrangel was advancing from the Andi Koysu, the troops gathered in Temir-Khan-Shura, having united with the Turchidag detachment under General Manyukin, ascended to the ridge enclosing the Koysubuli society from the eastern side and destroyed the mountain fortification of Burundluk-Kale. From the 22nd, the Koysubulians ceased to resist; the frontier fortress of Ulli-Kale opened its gates to us. General Manyukin garrisoned this fortress, as well as many points on the way, and began to build a crossing across the Avar-Koysu to open a direct communication between Baron Wrangel and Temir-Khan-Shura.

In a few days Avaria and Koysubu were brought under Russian control. Together with this peaceable population, the most hostile—the Gumbet population, which had been steadfastly in favor of Muridism since the day of its appearance in the Caucasus—was subdued. In Koysubu and Gumbet the popular government, which had been suppressed by Muridism, was restored. Rulership over Avaria, by prior permission of the tsar, was given to Ibrahim-Khan Mehtuli, the nearest relative of the extinct house of the Avars. The subjugated inhabitants immediately set up a militia against the Murids. In addition, with the conquest of the northwestern part of the mountains, the Dagestan detachment could have local means of transportation which the inhabitants willingly offered, thus greatly alleviating the main difficulty of mountain warfare: food for the troops. Local transports could move stores of provisions wherever they were needed without requiring any cover. With this aid, quickly and skillfully organized, the Dagestan detachment gained mobility that could not have been dreamed of before; the impassable terrain of the mountains opened up for them.

With the occupation of Koysubu and Avaria, the defensive line of the mountaineers fell by itself; the Dagestan detachment could come to its rear in two marches. On July 18th, Shamil galloped from Kilitlin mountain to Sogritlokh to verify whether the Russians were in fact crossing Koysu and saw with his own eyes our battalions on the right bank. From that moment, the Murid leader was left with two options: either lock himself in the blockades of the Kilitlin mountain, from which he had no way out, but where he could not be easily taken; or clear the banks of the Koysu and retreat with his entire army to Karata (which had become the capital of the mountains after the fall of Vedeno), before the crowd around him became more disorderly. Under the eyes of the imam the mountaineers would not lay down their arms, and Shamil could prolong his rule over the people for some time. But both options only showed Muridism's impotence before Russian arms. The news of the Avar and Koysubu submissions spread quickly over the mountains and aroused feelings that had long simmered in the hearts of the people; everyone began to think about his personal safety, refusing to sacrifice for a cause that was so clearly lost. The authorities established by Muridism had lost all significance in the eyes of the crowd. The people's party, which had been silent for thirty years against the spiritual despotism, suddenly stepped forward and took the upper hand. The political power of Muridism collapsed in three days.

From that moment on, the Russian camps were filled with former highland leaders and people's delegations. Significant men were hurrying over each other to declare their loyalty to the new power in the hope of preserving the position they had acquired; communities were hurrying to submit to rid themselves of the pogrom and supervision of the former chiefs, who had flown to the victor's headquarters. All those who had any status rushed to the nearest available power—to the commander-in-chief, Baron Wrangel, or Prince Melikov. Not much dignity and character were shown in this change by the men who for thirty years had amazed Russia with their unyielding firmness; but such phenomena are no longer usual in social upheavals of history, neither in Europe nor Asia.

When Shamil, after several days of hesitation, finally decided to retreat to Karata, the crowds he assembled no longer recognized any authority. People belonging to the subdued societies were the first to abandon the posts entrusted to them and return home; their example inspired others. Shamil had just moved down from the Kilitlin mountain, entrusting the defense of the fortress to one of the naibs, and the garrison occupying it looted the stores of provisions and scattered. From the several thousand mountaineers occupying the bank of the Koysu, only a few dozen now followed Shamil. The Karata people, despite their fortified terrain, refused to defend themselves. All means of resistance ran out for Shamil at once. Seeing his cause finally lost in northern Dagestan, he decided to rush to the southeast, to that belt of fortresses and the militant population, against which all Russian efforts had so far collapsed. The far-sighted imam had long ago prepared a refuge in this region, on the impregnable mountain Gunib. Having appeared in Andalal, Shamil could hope to keep in obedience the numerous and fanatical population of this country and if not to recover, at least to prolong affairs for an indefinite period of time. Andalal is enclosed by nature on all sides: on the south by snowy mountains, on the east and north by bottomless abysses in which three branches of the Koysu flow. The population of this part of the mountains is grouped in huge stone auls, each of which can withstand a proper siege. Having established himself in the middle of Andalal on the Gunib mountain, an impregnable position with excellent defenses, Shamil could maintain the determination of the surrounding population, attract throngs of fanatics and loyalists from all the mountains to Andalal, and put up a resistance against us which we would be powerless to break with any immediacy. The remnants of Muridism had only to keep their weapons in hand until the winter came. Our troops could not have continued the march through the snow-covered mountains because it was impossible to feed the horses, and Shamil would have remained face to face with the population that had trembled before his name for twenty-five years. In Andalal the outcome of the war was to be decided.

The conquest of Avaria reverberated in this region as it did in the others. A party hostile to Shamil came forward at once, headed by one of the founders of Muridism who spent a year fighting Shamil for supreme power, the famous Kibit-Magoma. Deprived of official importance but extremely influential in the mountains, this man attracted the population of Tibitl, one of the main Andalal auls, and sent a deputation to General Wrangel. The advocates of Muridism were, however, still strong in Andalal, and the other auls remained silent. The outcome of the matter depended on which party would prevail there. Having received the deputation of Kibit-Magoma, Baron Wrangel immediately moved Prince Tarkhanov, who stood on the eastern frontier of Dagestan, to the border of Andalal; however, after occupying so many points, there were very few men left in the Turchidag detachment. Prince Tarkhanov, known for his decisiveness, moved directly to Chokh, one of the main strongholds of Shamil, agitated the population of the aul, forced the Murids to flee from the fortress, and brought the Russian garrison into it. Despite this success, Chokh absorbed the last of his forces; he had nothing to proceed with. The other troops of the Dagestan detachment were scattered by a rapid invasion of Gumbet, Koysu, and Avaria; its right columns extended to Karat, to open communication with the Chechen detachment. Meanwhile Shamil rode away from Karata to Andalal with a few adherents. He was robbed twice on the road and driven back to the forests by Kibit-Magoma's men, but he managed to reach Gunib. The presence of the imam on the impregnable Gunib, in the middle of Andalal where the main auls had not yet shown obedience, again confused the matter and demanded the quickest measures.

Communication between the Dagestan and Chechen detachments via Karatu was opened on July 27th. Three days later, Adjutant General Baron Wrangel arrived in the main detachment. From both sides, the way deep into the mountains was open. The commander-in-chief decided to move all available forces on Andalal immediately, to suppress the adherents of the imam in this region before they had time to unite, and to surround Gunib closely, locking Shamil and the last of his Murids within. With our forces in sight, the party of Kibit-Magoma should have gained the upper hand in Andalal, but everything depended on the speed of action.

The commander-in-chief was confident that the newly subjugated population was pacified and could not, after such an abrupt change, again turn to the hostile camp in a few days. Relying on the energy, if not the loyalty, of the crowd, Prince Baryatinsky moved all the columns scattered across Avaria, Gumbet, Koysubu, and Kara-Koys to Andalal, leaving only a few companies in the newly conquered mountains to cover bridges and provision depots. The Chechen detachment sent a column through the Karata. The main difficulty with this unforeseen concentration of troops in the southwestern corner of the mountains was their food supply. The provisions for the Dagestan troops were in Salatavia; nothing was stocked within Andalal's borders. Emergency measures were taken immediately. Their energetic execution by the chief of staff of the Pre-Caspian region, Prince Mirsky, allowed the military operation to develop without the slightest loss of time; local means found

in the mountains, Chervodar transport, and regimental bun-
dles gathered by troops in Andalal were fed day by day
through the ridges of Gumbet, Koysubu, and Avaria; meanwhile convoys, formed abruptly in subdued Dagestan, carried the provisions stocked in the mountains to the nearest
points, from where, after the first days, the Andalal detachment would already have been adequately supplied.

With the entry of a considerable force into Andalal, the
party hostile to Shamil immediately triumphed. The whole
country and the surrounding mountain societies expressed
obedience to Baron Wrangel. Our troops closely encircled
Shamil, who had encamped with a few hundred desperate
men on the inaccessible summit of Gunib.

Having dispatched Adjutant General Wrangel to Andalal,
the commander-in-chief descended with a Chechen detachment into the Tekhnutsal valley on August 4th and set up
camp on the Andi Koysu, near the village of Konkhidatl by
the abandoned mountain fortifications. The next day General Prince Melikov, commander of the Lezgin line, arrived
at the Konkhidatl camp with his cavalry.

While the aforementioned events were taking place in
northern and western Dagestan, the Lezgin detachment was
advancing on the countries lying along the headwaters of
the Andi Koysu, in the barely passable mountains. Prince
Melikov embarked on the campaign earlier than the other
detachments. Having pulled the bulk of his troops together
at the foot of the Pokhalas-Tavi mountain, on July 6th he
started on the ridge, dividing the Didoi and Capuchin societies, setting up a wagon fort here and developing the road
to the Ilan-Khevi villages. At the same time, the side columns came out on the mountains at the two ends of the
Lezgin line: the Tushin column in the upper gorge of the
Andi Koysu, and the Zakatal column against the headwaters
of the Avar Koysu. Leaving any dead weight in the wagen-
burg, Prince Melikov moved to the Besho ridge and undertook from there a number of operations against the Lezgin
societies. He ravaged one by one the village of Kituri, which

had cost the life of General Vrevsky the previous year, the villages in the upper reaches of the Didoi tributaries of the Koysu, and the large aul Khupro, which had been rebuilt after the defeat of 1857.

In the meantime, the Tushino detachment brought the inhabitants of the upper gorge of Andi Koysu to submission and, advancing through the Didoi society and devastating the auls which lay in their way, joined Prince Melikov. Seeing no end to the devastation, many Lezgin villages began to surrender their properties. At this time, the movement that started in Avaria spilled over the mountains. Elected and significant people from all surrounding societies flocked to the camp of the Lezgin detachment. In a matter of days, the Didoi, Ilan-Khevi, Tindal, and Kvareshno societies were subdued. At the beginning of August, fulfilling the commander-in-chief's plan, Prince Melikov undertook a bold movement toward Tekhnutsal, through the snowy spurs of the Bokovoy range, breaching the depths of the region which had never before laid eyes on Russians. This campaign was accomplished with particular speed and precision. The Lezgin detachment reached the village of Tindi above the Andi Koysu. From there Prince Melikov continued his march with nothing but cavalry and came to Konkhidatl, passing between the Chechen society of Jamalal and the Lezgin Bogulaltsi, which Shamil had nicknamed his Siberia. Thus the unruly region was traversed in all directions. The three detachments that entered the mountains from different directions—northwest, northeast and south—came into contact, as it was intended, in the middle part of the Andi Koysu, relying on the central mass of the Chechen detachment. On his return from Konkhidatl, Prince Melikov was to move his detachment from the upper reaches of the Andi Koysu to the headwaters of the Avar, bringing the southern Lezgin communities into submission, occupy Irib—considered the main center of all the Lezgin region—and arrive at Gunib, where the commander-in-chief had appointed him a new rendezvous. As in the first half of the campaign, the operational lines of all active forces had to intersect at one point, determining the general direction of the campaign; now this point was moved from the middle of the Andi Koysu to the southeastern end of the mountains, in Andalal. Having laid a bridge fortification (named the Preobrazhensky) at the site of the camp, the commander-in-chief left on August 10th under cover of a small convoy to the troops concentrated in Andalal via Koysubu and Avaria. The Chechen detachment remained in Andia, under the command of General Kemfert, to complete the undertaken work.

The journey of the victor of the Caucasus through the conquered region had the character of a triumphal procession. He was greeted with speeches and addresses, salutes rang through the auls, and countless crowds flocked to look at him. Prince Baryatinsky rode through Avaria, which had been conquered only a fortnight before, not at the head of the troops, but as governor, with one convoy of a hundred; sometimes he was accompanied only by the locals. The mountaineers realized now that the war was truly over.

On August 18th, the commander-in-chief circled the Gunib mountain and arrived at Keger, the main headquarters of the Dagestan detachment. From there it was possible to see the whole of the Gunib mountain rising to the east, behind the Kara-Koysu cliff.

Gunib, aptly nicknamed the Guitar mountain by the soldiers, indeed has the (neckless) outline of this instrument, sloping from east to west, toward the left bank of the Kara-Koysu. It stands secluded among a cluster of surrounding mountains, dominating them. The slopes of Gunib are extremely steep, more than 45 degrees, and rise for a kilometer or more, ending with a sheer stone belt several dozen fathoms high which surrounds the entire hundred square kilometer area of the upper mountain; this belt is also raised above the inner wall, so that the very surface of the mountain forms a cup. At the foot of Gunib, the circumference of the mountain is about sixty kilometers. From the highest, eastern edge of the mountain, a small river flows down the slope and then cascades into the Koysu. On Gunib there is an aul and several farms, mills, birch groves, pastures, and arable fields—everything necessary to sustain human life. There is only one path leading to the mountain, from the shore of the Kara-Koysu, obscured for some distance by steep cliffs. Shamil blocked this area with a high wall full of loopholes. On the northern side, the crown of rocks, terminating the steep cliff, slides slightly in one place, leaving a narrow passage; the mountaineers barricaded it with debris, although there is no road there at all. On the other sides of the rocky belt there are a few rain-washed gullies, over which brave hunters have climbed with the help of a rope—but these passages appear quite inaccessible. If Shamil were capable of amassing sufficient force to occupy the entire upper circumference of Gunib with riflemen (requiring at least fifteen hundred men), this mountain would be truly impregnable. However, Shamil had only four hundred guns (including the population of the aul) and three cannons. Yet even with such meagre forces, the Gunib position was extremely strong; looking at the mountain, one could not find a good side to approach it from.

Shamil had only three or four men with him who were notable for their former positions. He brought with him to Gunib a small number of his domestic Murids, a few desperate Abreks, a few brutal followers of the tariqat, and a hundred fugitive soldiers, so burdened with crimes that they dared not take advantage of the forgiveness granted to them and turn themselves in alongside their comrades. The state created by Muridism, which fought against the Russian Empire for thirty years, began with a handful of fanatics and ended with a gang of brigands.

Even before the arrival of the commander-in-chief, Baron Wrangel had tightly encircled Gunib. All the paths leading to the floor of the mountain from the auls below were occupied by separate columns. On the eastern side, facing the interior of the mountain, the blockade was entrusted to Colonel Radetsky; the southeastern corner and the whole

southern side to Colonel Ter-Gukasov; the bank of the Koysu to Colonel Kononovich; and the northern side to General Prince Tarkhanov. The Murids who had encamped on
the mountain were hopelessly locked in.

On August 17th, Shamil sent representatives to Baron
Wrangel with an offer of ceasefire. The proposal was accepted. Upon the arrival of the commander-in-chief at the
Keger camp, negotiations of the surrender began immediately but led to nothing, despite the most generous terms
announced to Shamil and the complete security promised
to his men. The old leader of Muridism, obviously, was wavering between his lifelong conviction, which compelled
him to fight against the infidels to his last breath, and his
attachment to his large family, who were with him at Gunib;
besides, having grown up in implacable enmity to the Russians, he did not yet fully trust our promises. Shamil's final
words, which concluded the negotiations, were: "Gunib is a
high mountain; I am sitting on it. Above me, even higher, is
a god. The Russians are standing below. Let them storm it."

As the negotiations took place, General Prince Melikov
arrived at the Keger camp and performed the movement he
had been ordered to carry out. The Lezgin detachment went
deep into the mountains, from the upper reaches of the
Andi Koysu to the right bank of the Kara Koysu; brought to
submission the rest of the tribes of Lezgistan, which everywhere met our troops with cordiality; occupied Irib; and destroyed the fortifications of this aul. The eastern mountains
were conquered down to the last village, excepting Gunib,
on which the final remnants of Muridism were united.

On August 23rd the attack on Gunib was entrusted, under the chief command of Adjutant General Baron Wrangel,
to General Kesler, chief of engineers of the Caucasian army.
On the 24th, Prince Tarkhanov's column took the gardens
lying on the northern side of Gunib and positioned itself at
the foot of the mountain; Colonel Kononovich's column
came up from the Koysu riverbed and laid riflemen on the
first ledge of the bank. On the night of the 24th, it was

proposed to arrange bunkers for these two columns part-way up the mountain; but the troops, once thrown into battle, went on and on. While ascending the road, Colonel Kononovich met with the strongest resistance and had to halt. At the same time Colonel Ter-Gukasov, who stood against the southeastern corner of Gunib, having looked out beforehand for a large breach in the rocky belt crowning the mountain, rushed to it at dawn and by means of ropes and ladders ascended to the upper plain. Prince Tarkhanov feigned an attack during the night, which forced the Murids to throw down the piles of stones they had prepared. For two hours the mountain rumbled under the leaping fragments of rock. When this rain of stone was over, Prince Tarkhanov moved his columns upward to the breach—where the rocks of the ledge had been pushed apart—swept away the enemy's rubble, and stood on the mountain. Our troops now occupied the two opposite corners of Gunib. Most of the mountain's defenders were exterminated or taken. Shamil and the rest locked themselves in the aul at which all three columns were converging.

At noon, the commander-in-chief arrived at Gunib and demanded Shamil's immediate surrender. Fourteen battalions stood tightly around the small aul occupied by a hundred Murids. The remnant of the enemy had no opportunity either to leave or to fight back. After two hours of hesitation, the old imam left the aul and surrendered to the will of the victor.

The year, day, and hour of the end of the Caucasian War are carved in the birch grove, on the stone where Prince Baryatinsky sat and accepted the captive Shamil: "1859, August 25th, four o'clock in the afternoon."

Shamil was taken exactly three years later, to the day, from Prince Baryatinsky's appointment as commander-in-chief: August 25th, 1856.

Prince Baryatinsky informed the army about what had transpired in two consecutive orders. The first order was given on August 22th:

Warriors of the Caucasus! On the day of my arrival in the region I summoned you to gain great glory for our sovereign, and you have fulfilled my hope.

In three years you have conquered the Caucasus from the Caspian Sea to the Georgian Military Road.

May my loud thank you resound and pass through the defeated mountains of the Caucasus and may it penetrate with all the power of my soulful expression to your hearts.

The second order was issued on August 26:

Shamil is taken—I congratulate the Caucasian army.

During the leadership of Prince Baryatinsky, before his personal campaign, eight guns were taken from the mountaineers; during the final conquest of the mountains fifty-two guns were taken, totaling sixty guns in all. Our prisoners were released, more than two thousand of both sexes.

CONCLUSION

The eastern mountains are conquered forever. Such a phenomenon as Muridism is not repeated twice in the lifetime of a nation. But even Muridism, which expressed the ultimate degree of fanaticism of the most fanatical belief, which turned man himself into a passion, and which grew up on the most favorable soil that could be found in the world, united the mountaineers against us only because of circumstances that were absolutely exceptional. When the preaching of the tariqat began in the Caucasus, the depth of the mountains was still unknown and almost inaccessible; everything that took place there was hidden from our eyes. Without taking a good look at the character of the newly acquired region, the Russian authorities started operating with a faulty system, dismantling the original public institutions and scrapping the traditional systems which grew from the local soil and made every tribe cherish its independence; with their own hands, the Russian authorities broke the dams which Muridism would have struggled to breach. Then, for the convenience of external administration, they began to introduce Sharia law everywhere, surrendering the mountain population to the boundless influence of a doctrine hostile to us. As soon as Muridism, then still a small sect, had taken refuge in the mountains, the efforts of the Caucasian Corps were diverted to another direction, and for several years the advocates of the corrective tariqat enjoyed complete freedom in the eastern Caucasus. The highlanders of the 1830s had been prepared for centuries for the spiritual conflagration that suddenly engulfed the Caucasus. These richly gifted people lived only by immediate impressions, waiting for the first idea that would penetrate their minds. In the Caucasian mountaineers the properties of the two races that they delineate merge. With the passionate impressionability of the Asiatics they combine the energy, independence of personality, and enterprise of the Europeans, which so sharply distinguish them from their relaxed coreligionists who live behind them to the very edge of the Asian continent. For the mountaineers, Muridism appealed to both sides of their nature, creating for them an ideal life that required no moral effort on the part of man, consisting of battles, adventures, dangers, and plunder, crowned with paradise. As long as it was necessary only to act, the mountaineers flocked under the banners of the imam with unparalleled zeal. But when Muridism began to organize their life on the basis of Sharia and imposed religious guardianship on them, they turned against it. Left to themselves, eye to eye with the Sharia, the mountaineers could not stand the Muslim character. In a few days the religious dimension of Muridism would disappear from popular memory; only legend would remain about it as a great struggle of the Caucasian tribes against the Russians. Now, with the fall of Muridism, the mountain population has again broken up into separate tribes. The ancient folk institutions already partly restored, with adaptions made to accommodate the needs of the Russian power, will eventually be made clear and formally legalized.

The eastern Caucasus, divided into two large regions—the left flank and the Pre-Caspian region—is subdivided into eleven districts; in each district there should be a court and justice according to custom, made up of people's elders and elected officials. The societies that make up the districts are governed by naibs chosen from honorable locals who are loyal to us. This way of governing, first established in Chechnya by Prince Baryatinsky during his command of the left flank, was justified by long experience. The newly subjugated Chechens stood firmly with us even in the face of a struggle that remained uncertain; their country was relatively safe, while it was impossible to pass without an armed escort through the lands of other societies that had already been subjugated for half a century.

In the Caucasus, popular self-government based on clearly defined rights, with the elimination of a spiritual influence, preserves the tranquility of the region better than thousands of bayonets. As the shots were silenced in different parts of the Caucasus, the brave but hungry population of the mountains laid down their guns and eagerly began peaceful labor. With the development of the people's welfare, new social needs not satisfied by the ancient custom will surely arise and will themselves cause the gradual introduction of enlightened legislation. The interior of the mountains is being actively opened by convenient roads. For the last three years, our troops have been moving forward with nothing but a shovel and an axe in their hands; where they have passed, it is now possible to travel on wheels along what were once mountain paths. Roads in the mountains are like windows in a house; they let in the light from outside.

In a year's time the whole of the eastern Caucasus will be partitioned by man-made roads in all directions; the crossings will be enclosed by small, close fortifications, requiring only a few companies of garrison for the entire country. The Caucasus will be subdued because it will be accessible in all its depths and from all sides. Moreover, the warlike population of the mountains will become their own security. The troops recruited from the natives served as faithfully as

Russian troops—a fact that has long been known in the Caucasus—and they are much more effective than the latter for guarding peace in the mountains. The native squads, attracting to themselves the most determined youth, are endowed in the eyes of the mountain population not only with material advantages, but also with great moral power, which they dare not oppose; these squads will form a link between the mountain tribes and the Russian power. A long and fierce war had developed the already-bellicose spirit of the Caucasian tribes too much not to allow an outlet for it; there were too many people in the mountains, accustomed to feeding themselves with weapons alone, to leave them to starve without occupation. These very people—Kachags, Abreks, brigands of all names who made the mountain region impassable for a hundred kilometers around—having joined the mountain squads as hunters, will be faithful soldiers (as proven by the Dagestan cavalry regiment, the best police in the mountains) and an excellent army for external warfare. To maintain tranquility in the mountains, settled and uncovered, would require very few troops. The Caucasus, which has hitherto absorbed half of the active forces of the empire, will soon become a source of new strength for it.

The conquest of the eastern mountains has abruptly changed the defensive and offensive position of the Caucasian army. From the present year, the isthmus between the Black Sea and the Caspian Sea has been forever secured to Russia, whatever political combinations may take place in neighboring countries, whatever forces may be directed against the Caucasus. Yet so far the empire has only secured possession of the isthmus. Much remains to be done to arrange it as it should be, so that it may be quite in harmony with the aims and endowments of the state. Only after a few years of strenuous effort, with unrelenting means, will it be possible to say, "It's ready!"

The first task to be accomplished in the Caucasus, a task which must be finished as soon as possible, is the conquest

of the western mountains. With the fall of Shamil, the rear
of the Caucasian army is secured and its scattered forces
are gathered; but neither of these things is quite complete,
as long as the governor-general of Kutaisi is separated from
the Kuban line by a wide belt of unruly mountains and as
long as a considerable mass of troops is immovably confined to one part of the region. The mere possibility of
fighting against the Russian Empire, in whatever remote
corner of the country the struggle may take place, inevitably
keeps the whole population in a state of anxiety and kindles
hopes which would not otherwise exist. Such an example is
all the more dangerous in a Muslim land. Besides, the unruly
Adyghes own the shore of the sea, which opens to them
communication with the whole world. I do not at all share
the opinion that the land of the Adyghes should be considered a gate into the heart of the Caucasus to be opened in
the event of an enemy invasion. It is as difficult for allies to
pass through this land as for enemies; besides, volatile
Ubykhs or Shapsugs can only be one's allies for three days.
Even without outside support, existence of an open enemy
between the Kuban and Abkhazia is quite burdensome and
dangerous. Now, with the fall of eastern mountains, the
struggle in the Caucasus is morally resolved. The Adyghes
cannot hold out against the active strength which the Caucasian army possesses for long; but only against *such*
strength. Reducing the army before the country has been
completely pacified would again prolong the matter in the
Caucasus and ultimately cost much more for the resulting
complexity than forceful, short-term actions. If in 1816,
with the appointment of General Yermolov to the Caucasus,
several regiments returning from abroad were assigned to
him, the empire would have avoided a thirty-year war with
Muridism and reduced its losses by hundreds of millions of
rubles and hundreds of thousands of people. The western
mountains must be conquered without delay, sparing no
sacrifice.

The second thing which is necessary for the Caucasus

both militarily and socially, for the army and for the region as a whole, is the construction of the Transcaucasian railroad. I cannot develop this matter here—which has already been discussed by the authorities—as such a development would require another book of the same size, but I will outline its main features. If in the recent war the fate of the country was decided on the field of battle by nine battalions, it was due as much to the absorption of our forces by highland warfare as to the extreme slowness of communications, which compelled us to scatter our troops at all points where the enemy might appear—for we had no other way to get there in time. In the Caucasus, with the meandering outline of the border which includes both land and sea, there are several lines leading straight from the circumference to the center; lines, the possession of which can strategically decide the fate of the war. Food had to be procured long in advance, with the greatest difficulty, in accordance with the original disposition of the troops, which could not be changed afterward because of the impossibility of moving the stores. The troops were confined to their provision depots, even though military circumstances sometimes produced quite different needs; hence the fragmentation and weakness of the army, which on the whole was quite significant. In order to make the strength of Russian troops in Transcaucasia both defensively and offensively correspond to their actual number, it is necessary to cut through the region with a railway line from sea to sea. Then the Transcaucasian troops, which have been so far weak due to their fragmentation, will form one body capable of dealing an irresistible blow in any direction. With the rapid development of the Volga and Caspian shipping companies, Transcaucasia, connected into one entity by the railway, will become at all its points a three-week journey to the main centers of the state, and thus become part of the general composition of the Russian regions. Instead of the numerous army which now, even in peace time, has to be kept in this remote frontier region, Transcaucasia will only have to be heavily occupied in times of war, like any other part of the frontier; requiring forces proportional to the actual danger, and not to any possible accident, as is currently the case when the mountainous region is half a year's journey from the interior of Russia.

The savings for the state will be enormous, its power on the side of the Caucasian isthmus will triple, and at the same time the Caucasian army will become mobile, like all the active troops of the empire. The railroad will have the same influence on the welfare of the country as irrigation has on fertile but sun-burned soil. Until now, all the natural forces of Transcaucasia slept in the ground; the only consumer here was the treasury. The railroad will make these regions, which so far have brought nothing but expenses, an independent and wealthy part of the empire. Finally, the railway line from Baku to Poti, which crowns our position in the Caucasus, is economically much more secured than any of the Russian lines which will have to excite and attract traffic that does not yet exist; the 25 million rubles worth of goods that annually flood Persia and all of upper Asia through Trabzon are only waiting for a convenient path through Transcaucasia and the Caspian Sea. At the present time this trade is making its way through the most inhospitable country, the high mountainous area of Turkish Armenia, transported on pack animals and without roads. A railroad between the two seas will draw this trade to itself and double the quantity of goods, reducing their selling price. The cost of the railroad, according to the calculations already made, will only slightly exceed the cost of the Russian lines; the value of the cargo of the Trabzon trade should more than recoup this sum, even at high interest rates. This enterprise, necessary politically and militarily, is at the same time profitable economically.

With the conquest of the western mountains and the establishment of a railroad between the Black and Caspian seas, the Caucasian army will become part of the active forces of the empire. It is still impossible to determine even approximately how much this return of two hundred thousand soldiers (perhaps the first in the world), excluded so far from the total of Russian forces, will elevate the military power of the state. The incessant and merciless war has shaped several generations in the Caucasus who are trained in the martial craft almost hereditarily. A new recruit, having joined a Caucasian regiment and having not yet seen the enemy, gets used to the idea of war as a natural and everyday business of life; having undertaken several campaigns, he develops personally, not only as a soldier, but as a fighter. He continually meets the enemy one on one—on a forest trail, on a mountain path, in a besieged village—and gets used to relying on himself alone, on his nerve and his gun. When a column of these men forms, with each absolutely confident in himself, they become so convinced of their invincibility that only a disproportionate material force can resist them. We have seen enough examples of this in the past war.

This kind of education was previously given only to the ancient armies, where every soldier was a fighter, and it was completely forgotten in the European armies from the moment when the duty of a soldier became only to march *en masse* behind his banner and listen to commands. A Caucasian soldier is like an officer in his own way. Russian valor needs a broad field; in peacetime it is only in the Caucasus that arms rattle, beckoning men with military inclinations. Young officers whose hearts are attracted to the fighting life gradually flock to the Caucasus by themselves. The mountain war quickly develops their military instinct, makes a real leader out of an officer, one who is able to manage people and control battles. In the forest and in the mountains, no matter how numerous the detachment may be, the company commander becomes an isolated leader; he is left to conduct an almost independent business, in which his character and disposition receive independent rights, and he becomes one of the causes of general success or failure.

The responsibility for military decisions reaches much

lower ranks in the Caucasus than in European warfare, and the men who are put before the daily reckoning of experience are sorted out by themselves. Moreover, special circumstances of life and actions have developed in the Caucasian regiments: the spirit of a military family, the pride in their regimental uniform and their banner—always justified by some high military quality which the regiment has acquired exclusively for itself. The relationship of mutual responsibility between people of all degrees flourished here more than any other army, and naturally instilled in the individual full confidence in his unit, due to the ability to rely on each of its constituent people. Continuous campaigns hardened the Caucasian soldier, made him the greatest foot soldier in the world, taught him to live anywhere and with anything. The Caucasian War formed an army for Russia, which, under its banner, is ready to consider itself at home at the edge of the world, which immediately understands every application of military affairs, and which the enemy must exterminate in order to defeat. When a Caucasian battalion faces the enemy, it considers as a battle only the time it needs to run to the enemy's lines; this confidence is shared by all its ranks, from the commander to the drummer.

In addition to the regular army, the Caucasian War has nurtured for Russia another excellent and unique force— the Linear and Black Sea Cossacks. Equally capable of close formation and horsemanship, cavalry and infantry, when used in large numbers these men, fearless, indefatigable, fast as the wind, can carry out aspects of military affairs hitherto unheard of: blocking the enemy army in its own country, disuniting it, encircling it from the rear and flanks, breaking communication between separate columns. Until now, the Linear Cossacks had participated only as a part of divisions in European warfare; yet even there, they left a lasting impression. With the end of the Caucasian War, over forty thousand Cossacks could join the army. This remarkable army expressed aspects of the Russian nature that go unnoticed in civilian life. The best line regiments were formed before our eyes, from villagers; to such an extent that the spirit of the Cossacks still lives, if not in the mind, then in the blood of the Russian man. In a few years these villagers, placed on the enemy's border, became the bravest and most dexterous horsemen, true Abreks, superior to the Chechens, and at the same time obedient, fully disciplined soldiers, capable of all kinds of service. So quickly did the military spirit develop in these villagers that in a few years a young woman, yesterday's peasant, would not want to say a kind word to a Cossack who was not considered a brave soldier. Russia, with its immense size, still lives the life of different centuries. In the Ukrainian lands—Caucasian, Siberian, Kyrgyz—Cossacks still exist in the same condition as they existed in the sixteenth century on the Dnieper and the Don. Simultaneously warriors and villagers, Cossacks develop the land they occupied with arms in their hands, bring the Russian fatherland into foreign deserts, and should be for the empire what American pioneers are for the United States. In the Caucasus it would have been impossible to deal with the mountaineers without the settlement of the front lines by Cossacks. Before long the Caucasian Cossack regiments will be advanced further ahead and the Cossack population, reinforced by newcomers, will increase considerably. Then not forty, but maybe seventy thousand Caucasian Cossacks could be ready to take up their banners at the first call of the fatherland.

The third element of the new strength that the conquered Caucasus lends to the empire lies in the mountain troops. Under the system now adopted, their number can be great, and their quality cannot be doubted. There can be no better troops than the Dagestan cavalry regiment and the Anapa squadron. For Caucasian mountaineers, battles and peril are as essential as for the ancient Scandinavians. It is only necessary to provide the right outlet for their warlike nature, and then the Caucasus can throw out of its depths the units which will surprise the world under Russian banners.

The conquest of the eastern Caucasus cost the empire great sacrifices; the conquest of the western will cost still more, perhaps for some time. But this conquest will be accomplished in the shortest possible time and the natural and personal forces of the country will be properly developed; in this you can trust a man whom the whole Caucasus, a good judge of practical men, trusted from the moment he stepped foot there. With the definitive pacification of the isthmus, this part of the Russian Empire will amply reward the state politically and militarily, and in part even economically. The mere return of the Caucasian army to the total of our active forces, and the cessation of fruitless sacrifices and ever-present apprehension over this country, constitute a success of great importance. We may reasonably think that if the mountains had been pacified in 1853, the war would have taken a very different turn. Now, at least, this great deed has been accomplished; the fulfillment of the rest, with the same strong administration, can be calculated ahead with certainty. The establishment of undisputed Russian rule on the Caucasian isthmus, fully organized, will be a world event whose consequences will not be exhausted for several generations. At the present time it is not yet possible to comprehend with human judgment all that may develop from the final conquest of the Caucasus, this bridge from the Russian shore into the heart of the Asiatic continent. The future is not within the power of man, but men have the power to be worthy of a great future. For the time being, as long as we are satisfied with what has been accomplished, we will say with Bohdan Khmelnytsky: "What will be will be, and what will be will be God's will."

ENJOYED THIS BOOK?

TO READ MORE, VISIT US AT

ANTELOPEHILLPUBLISHING.COM